ALSO BY HÉCTOR TOBAR

Fiction

The Last Great Road Bum

The Barbarian Nurseries

The Tattooed Soldier

Nonfiction

Deep Down Dark: The Untold Stories of 33 Men Buried in a
Chilean Mine, and the Miracle That Set Them Free

Translation Nation: Defining a New American Identity
in the Spanish-Speaking United States

OUR MIGRANT SOULS

OUR MIGRANT SOULS

A Meditation on Race
and the Meanings and Myths of "Latino"

HÉCTOR TOBAR

MCD · FARRAR, STRAUS AND GIROUX

NEW YORK

MCD
Farrar, Straus and Giroux
120 Broadway, New York 10271

Printed in the United States of America
First edition, 2023

Photograph on title-page spread courtesy of the author.

Library of Congress Cataloging-in-Publication Data
Names: Tobar, Héctor, 1963– author.
Title: Our migrant souls : a meditation on race and the meanings and
    myths of "Latino" / Héctor Tobar.
Other titles: Meditation on race and the meanings and myths of "Latino"
Description: First edition. | New York : MCD / Farrar, Straus and
    Giroux, 2023.
Identifiers: LCCN 2022055249 | ISBN 9780374609900 (hardcover)
Subjects: LCSH: Hispanic Americans—Ethnic identity. | Hispanic
    Americans—Social conditions. | Immigrants—United States—
    Social conditions. | United States—Race relations.
Classification: LCC E184.S75 T62 2023 | DDC 305.868/073—
    dc23/eng/20230111
LC record available at https://lccn.loc.gov/2022055249

Our books may be purchased in bulk for promotional, educational, or
business use. Please contact your local bookseller or the Macmillan
Corporate and Premium Sales Department at 1-800-221-7945, extension
5442, or by email at MacmillanSpecialMarkets@macmillan.com.

www.mcdbooks.com • www.fsgbooks.com
Follow us on Twitter, Facebook, and Instagram at @mcdbooks

10 9 8 7 6 5 4 3 2 1

This is a work of nonfiction. The names and identifying characteristics
of some individuals have been changed to protect their privacy.

For Dr. Vicki L. Ruiz,
and the many historians she has mentored

CONTENTS

PROLOGUE: OUR MIGRANT SOULS 3

PART I: OUR COUNTRY

1. EMPIRES 15

2. WALLS 26

3. BEGINNINGS 43

4. CITIES 54

5. RACE 74

6. INTIMACIES 93

7. SECRETS 114

8. ASHES 128

9. LIES 141

PART II: OUR JOURNEYS HOME

10. LIGHT 169

11. HOME 195

CONCLUSION: UTOPIAS 223

Acknowledgments 243

OUR MIGRANT SOULS

OUR MIGRANT SOULS

You write words for me to read, a string of memories that place me inside the eyes of the child you were. A daughter of Honduras. Of Mexico and of Puerto Rico, and of the Central Valley of California, with its flat, dry plains covered with crops and cows, and towns filled with paisas and their chickens. You sit in my office and begin to weep as you tell me the story of your undocumented boyfriend and the demons that haunt him, and it is clear to me that you should break up with him, even though I cannot say this. You tell me about your best friend, a white girl, and about the African American family who lived next door. In your stories I see a suburb of rectangular lawns, and a "rancho" in the rural United States, where the neighbors heard your mother and father yelling at each other, and where you took solace in the natural beauty of your surroundings, in the crisp desert wind and the muddy yellow outline of mountain ranges. You write, "I am having a nervous breakdown," but your prose belies this; controlled and precise, it tells a story of violation and survival you endured when you were a kindergartner.

I read the pages you write for me and I learn that, as a child, you were the good daughter who helped raise her siblings. You were the son who worked alongside your father in his landscaping business; you were the daughter who rubbed your father's weary feet every night. And you recount the months you were living in your car, with your parents and brother, taking "baths" at night at the spigot outside a laundromat; you describe the water flowing over your "butt cheeks" in a way I'll never forget. When your parents were depressed and nearly broken, you kept the home together. You witnessed your mother disappear to confront your father's lover, and you watched the home invaders who arrived in your living room, criminals speaking poor Spanish with their children in tow. You cooked and you drove siblings to doctors' appointments, and now I see you sitting before me, your sense of humor intact, an awareness and a dignity and a purpose about you. In a minute, you will become frazzled, but fifteen minutes later, you will recover yourself. Your eyes dart nervously, and then, suddenly, I see the centered you and I want to weep because I can see you walking into the future, unbroken.

Your coloring, the shape of your nose, and the raven locks that drop over your forehead suggest the world and its variety. An African heritage. Your indigeneity. Your Europeanness. You are everything—and you are the very specific places your parents came from. You are Texas and Oaxaca and Andalusia, and villages with burros and concrete cities covered in wires and digital signals. Like my own DNA, yours is a cipher of secrets and chance encounters and migrations. Your story passes through Guatemala and Compton, it has side routes into Tennessee and North Carolina. You describe bringing home your African

American boyfriend, and your Mexican father gazing up at him and saying, with admiration, "Es alto el cabrón." You gaze back into your history, and you show me market towns in Central American valleys that straddle rivers lined with ceiba trees. "Ethnicity" and "race" are sold to us as boxes containing our skin tones and our surnames, but the truth about you, about us, will not fit in any box. You have the labels "undocumented" and "Mexican" and "Cubana" attached to you, and yet English is your mother tongue and your favorite band is the Smiths. You were born in the United States but you can speak Zapotec. You describe, again and again, how terrible you feel about your Spanish, or your lack of it, because Spanish is this language that's supposed to bind us to our people and our past. You are a deep brown and you are fair-skinned, your eyes are black and they are green, and you are nineteen, and twenty, and twenty-one, and you are brilliant in the same way your mother and father were. Those sharp-eyed, impulsive, and impatient border crossers who begot you. Barrio math wizards who dropped out of school in the sixth grade. "My mother is a savant," you tell me. Never formally educated, still undocumented, she builds a jewelry empire with your father. Your parents sell tacos one day, and decades later, they own a horse ranch. From the kitchen at a Chinese fast-food restaurant, to bartering at the swap meet, to the chain holding the keys to their own business.

But you are hurt, today. So many hateful words have been spoken about us. Ancient tropes, crude insults tossed carelessly into the stream of images and voices of the modern age. This country posits us as an uneducated people, as servers and brawn, as cleaners of floors and toilets, picking up the trash. We are the laboring backdrop to this country's affluence. Our humanity and our complexity exist outside broadcast and printed culture, rarely as alive and full as I see in your writing. I read your account of your mother's solitary journey to California, and the apartment where she lived with eighteen people, and your father's stubborn efforts to court her; he never did quite succeed in sweeping her off her feet. You describe family wreckage and pride and alcoholism and the joys of first kisses and what it's like to still live in the closet and how much it hurt when your ignorant tía said those things about women who love other women. You are the daughter whose mother never caught her fooling around with her güerita girlfriend in her bedroom, under the covers during "sleepovers"—until she read your journal. Now you write words for me to read, in this place of learning where you came in search of useful knowledge that will bring sense to the conflict and disorder around you. You want the power of printed words and ideas to flow through your veins for the rest of your days. This is why you have sought me out. Your eyes drift to the books on the shelves in my office, each one representing learning and reason, the power of studied truths, revealed.

And this, indeed, is what I want to give you. I see you, ten rows back, during my lecture on Central American and Caribbean history in the twentieth century. I am showing slides of dictators in epaulets, and guerrilla fighters wearing secondhand T-shirts exported to El Salvador from the Goodwills of the United States, and the papery leaves of drought-stricken cornfields, and boys and girls with the bloated bellies of malnutrition. I show you the logos of the United States companies that transformed our homelands into "banana republics." And I say: "We think we're a fucked-up people, but it's this history that's fucked up. All this violence inflicted upon us: that is what haunts us . . ." As I speak, I see you, ten rows back, wiping away a tear, and I think: I came into this world, and I mastered words and studied history, just so I could stand here before you, Diana, Isaac, Andrea, Elizabeth, Christián, Delia. So that I could show you the hurt, the daring, and the beauty to be found in our shared histories. The women who gave their bodies to the Mexican Revolution, the gender-fluid soldadera who led troops into battle in her leather pants. I've come here, after decades of study, so that I could see you sit up straight in the lecture hall, a smile forming on your lips now, because in the scroll of knowledge I have opened for you, you see a truth that's always been there, around you, inside you, unspoken.

This is my mission now. Here, in my own pages, which are meant to honor your stories and add to them, I will weave what I know with what you have taught me, and together we will arrive at an understanding of our times, and our "people." And we will be stronger and ready for the next fight, and the one after that, and all the many struggles to come.

I HAVE THREE CHILDREN WHO ARE ABOUT THE SAME AGE AS you. My wife and I raised them in the years and decades when racist ideas about people of Latin American descent were spreading across the United States. We wanted them to be strong and happy inside their skins. As with many people of my generation, and yours, the spread of intolerance across our country only made us more determined and defiant to take pride in everything that made us "primitive" to and despised by the ignorant and the ill-informed.

For us, as for most "Latino" families, our fortitude is grounded in the realization that we are on a journey that is generations long. Our ancestors look back at us from old black-and-white photographs and from the faded Polaroids of the last century, and in their steely expressions, or their old-country optimism, we see a shield in a world of cruel judgments. In our history we see the germ of the human worth, beauty, and dignity of our people.

But what does it mean to say we are a "people"? What do we pass on to our children when we call ourselves Latino, or its many synonyms? Truth be told, those of us who can call ourselves "Latino" feel ridiculous half the time we use the term. "Latino," "Latinx," and "Hispanic" all have European roots. As such, they erase our Indigenous and African past. And they are repeated so often in superficial reports in the United States media (where few Latino faces are visible) that they can feel as fake and artificial as a marketing slogan, or a cartoon.

"Latino," "Latinx," and "Hispanic" are terms that are said to describe our "ethnicity," or "common cultural background." In practice, however, the rest of the country treats us as a "race." Police transmissions describe "Hispanic male" suspects, and news reports list "Latino" alongside the races "white," "Black," "Native American," and "Asian" when discussing the demographics of the United States. Behind these categories is the belief that "race" is a biological subdivision of the species *Homo sapiens*, and that the members of the same race are similar in more ways than just skin color. Racist ideas about "Latino" people are tied to the belief that we are born into a lower caste, and that, as a people, we are inconsequential in the American story. This is not just an attitude held by "white" people, as one Asian American student reminded me. At a time when many of my students were writing about the wave of anti-Asian hate during the COVID-19 pandemic, he told me the story of his Hong Kong immigrant family and the mother who scolded the son who became a car mechanic instead of going to college. She told him: "You might as well be Mexican."

Many a Latino parent has felt the shroud of racial prejudice hovering over their children. We think of our progeny and their brilliant minds, their brightness and their eagerness as they go into the world, and the way strangers will dismiss them, or not see them, because of the stereotypes attached to our people. I've watched my children fight, as I've seen you fight, to assert their intelligence and creativity and willfulness against the smallness and the stupidity of those who see us through a race lens.

Race is an invention of long-dead ideologues and long-discredited scientists who collected skulls and told fairy tales about them. Perhaps you have sensed this already, as you walk about the culturally diverse spaces of North America. Real human beings and their bodies and their faces and their idiosyncrasies don't fit into the coloring books that the United States has created to illustrate what race means. Race is a story we tell ourselves about one another. In the case of people of Latin American descent, that story was born from a history of conquest and exploitation, and from our own acts of resistance to exploitation and prejudice. You and I, and countless authors and activists, use "Latino" or "Latinx" or "Hispanic" to express an alliance among peoples, a shared experience. But in the intimate spaces of your friendships and your homes, you are not inclined to use these terms. When you are asked the annoying question "What are you?" you are more likely to answer with something more specific and more satisfying, something closer to your lived experience. "I'm Mexican," you might say, even if you were born in the United States; or, "my father's Salvadoran and my mother's Irish"; or, "I'm from a mixed-status family"; or, "I'm Nuyorican." Or you might say, as many of my students have said over the years, "I'm from South Central L.A.," or, "I'm Blaxican," because your identity has been born of the contact between people of African American and Latin American descent, something common in all the cities of the United States.

Like the other racial and ethnic terms in this country, "Latino" and "Hispanic" were created as counterpoints to "white." To call a human being "white" itself is strange, if you consider the literal meaning of the word. "White" and its antonym, "Black," are abstractions applied to people whose skin colors are, truly, various shades of the most common color in the animal kingdom, brown. Americans popularized the terms "Black," "red," and "yellow" to describe races other than "white," and Latino people are often referred to as "brown." "White" was invented five hundred years ago to describe the privilege enjoyed by one group of people, and to justify the exploitation of "Black" people. In the words of James Baldwin, "White is a metaphor for power." And today, it remains both an assertion of racial superiority and a declaration of a twisted notion of freedom. To be white is to have entered a world free of the pain of history, an abstract space where opportunity and individualism rule. The racial and ethnic labels of the United States are old and imprecise and illogical; and yet they dominate our lives in the present. They are outlined in civil rights laws, counted as census categories, and are used to determine our admission to universities, and they can determine the length of our jail sentences. As more than one commentator has said, race is a gun from the past being pointed at the heads of people living in the present.

The relationship of Latino people to North American ideas about race is one more chapter in this country's convoluted and contradictory race story. Latino people can think of themselves as white, and many of our unenlightened relatives believe lighter skin makes them superior human beings. In the most recent U.S. census, one-fifth of us chose "white" as our race. And yet a powerful media and political elite has convinced millions of United States residents that the problem of brown people of Latin American descent is the great, existential race threat of our times. We are, in their thinking, murderers, drug dealers, and welfare parasites. They have convinced many "white" Americans that impregnable barriers must be built at the Mexican border to protect them from the barbarism of Latin America and its mestizo and Indigenous masses.

A farcical and inhuman history turned us into "brown" people and "Hispanics" and "illegal aliens" and "spics." But when we spend time living inside that history, and untangling the roots of the racist ideas about us, we can feel stronger and more centered. We can see that the insults directed at us have increased the more dependent the country has become on our labor. This country's wealth and power have been built upon our personal ambitions and the intimacies of our families. We have become the scaffolding of the United States, its plumbing, its daily meal, the roof over the head of its children. Your parents cooking dinner in their favorite sartén and olla, and your guardian serving you scrambled eggs in the morning, and the weddings and graduations they celebrate with pictures on their living room walls: all of that is part of the essence of the United States of America. Our stories, and their Latin American threads, are woven inside the story of the United States, alongside the narratives of people like Dred Scott and Wong Kim Ark, a Black man and a Chinese American whose travails helped give many of us our citizenship.

We can begin the exploration of our "identity" by understanding the connections between this larger story and the communities that have formed us. My California barrio and your Main Street and your Calle Morelos, your Broadway, your rancho, your Malecón, your neighborhood basketball court, your Sexta Avenida, your freeway off-ramp, your Westgate Mall, your apartment building and your park, and all the people who putter about and work and love in these places. These communities may seem uninteresting, or common—even more so if they are the places where we've lived most of our lives. But chances are that if we scrape away a few years, a decade or two, if we look into the local archives, if we begin to query the minds of the people who live in these places, we will find stories and riddles, and strange coincidences, and the beginning of an understanding of the deep matrix of human history to which we belong.

There are several communities in my family's journey. But the one I know best is a metropolis on the Pacific Ocean, and neighborhoods where jade plants grow and palm trees bend as they age. The awakening of my own consciousness begins here; this is where my wife and I raised our children into adulthood. This is the place I've worked hardest to understand, to unlock the code buried in the sidewalks and hidden in the street signs, the city where I learned to walk, and to speak two languages at once, a city whose name itself is synonymous with mystery, injustice, and possibility.

PART I **OUR COUNTRY**

1

EMPIRES

My children grew up devouring stories of empire and injustice, fantasies set in worlds that are not our own. I took them to movies and bought them books that transported them into fictional realms and into alternate pasts, or deep into the future, or into a galaxy "far, far away." This is a rite of passage of a United States childhood. We watch and read narratives of powerful elites living inside stone towers and walled cities, protected by death rays and roiling fires and all-seeing eyes. The empire of fantasy and cosplay is steel and stone perfection, and it is savagery. We sit in a darkened theater, or with our faces covered in the bluish glow of our private screens, and we watch heroes who are small and weak and isolated fight back against power. When we see the empire defeated, we feel strong, liberated, and renewed.

Stories about empire move us because they're echoes of the memories that reside deep in our collective consciousness. We live in a world of migrating peoples and interconnected markets, a global system of wealth creation built upon acts of violence. In the Americas, European conquerors erased ways of life that were alien to them, fought wars, enslaved people, razed temples, and outlawed religions. Bits and pieces of this history have been passed down to us. In class, or in books, we learn about the ship with captive men and women from the African kingdom of Ndongo that arrived in the colony of Virginia in 1619; about the Cherokee, Chickasaw, Choctaw, Muscogee, and Seminole being forced out of their lands in the Trail of Tears. Hollywood takes the history of colonialism and conquest and dresses up the characters in robes and helmets and gives them prop weapons, and it transforms this history into a crowd-pleasing fantasy. As Junot Díaz once put it: without the history of racialist ideologies, *X-Men* makes no sense; without colonialism, *Star Wars* make no sense; and without the history of chattel slavery in the New World, *Dune* makes no sense.

The largest "Latino" city in the United States, Los Angeles, is also the home of a movie and television industry that makes billions of dollars telling empire fantasy stories. The most recent film adaptation of *Dune* earned more than $400 million in box office revenue, and when I saw the film with my Mexican Guatemalan American son (who had read the novel in high school), we listened as one of the characters pronounced a speech about the horrors inflicted by an empire. Her words could have been spoken by any of a number of different peoples across the eons of time: "The outsiders ravage our lands in front of our eyes. Their cruelty to my people is all I've known."

In the real lives of Latino families, the empire's power is plain to see. Let's start with geography, and the natural barriers that separate the beginning and the present of our family stories. The choppy seas of the Straits of Florida and the western Atlantic; the cacti and dry washes and dirt trails in the Sonoran Desert. The United States Coast Guard patrols the migrant routes across the Caribbean, and along the border between Mexico and California and Arizona there are fences, and a wall. What is a barrier several hundred miles long, topped with barbed wire and patrolled by armed guards, but the physical expression of an empire and its will?

The idea of Latino or Hispanic people as a race apart was born from the history of the United States and its triumphant march across the North American continent. The United States made us into "people of color," and now our American story has the epic sweep of an IMAX movie; we have crossed oceans and deserts, and entered into new and exotic urban "barrios" and "ghettos," and planted roots in farm towns on vast and verdant plains. Armies, police, and various systems of incarceration enforce an unequal order in which our labor produces the riches of an empire. Many of us live with the everyday fear that the agents of the empire will arrive at our front doors and take our mothers and fathers and grandparents away from us, into an imperial machinery of detention and deportation.

In trying to subjugate us, the empire *darkens* us, in more than one sense of that word. *Melanin* is what makes us darker, and *melancholy* is a darkening of the spirit. The root of these two words is the same: the Greek "melas," meaning black. Throughout this country's history, the lives of the people today known as "Latino" have been shaped by the American tradition of creating legal categories applied to the "nonwhite." We have been "braceros" and "illegal aliens" and "resident aliens," and for many of us migration to the United States has become a one-way journey, a forever-goodbye to our homelands. Our second-class, outsider status in the United States produces the melancholy that is, in many ways, a defining element of the migrant experience. "Did he know he was never going to see his own mom and dad ever again?" one of my students writes of her immigrant father's departure from Mexico. "Did he know that twenty years later he would cry like a small child for his mom"—watching on a video call from California—"as his sisters and brothers, aunts and uncles, buried her frail corpse . . ."

The experience of having been uprooted from one way of life and transported into another, entirely different way of living marks the collective psyche of Latino people in the real-life empire of the United States of America. We have an ancestor who left behind a home where she understood the ways of the world, where she knew the paths across her village to take to school and work, where she knew the names of her neighbors and the moods and light of the changing seasons. She enters a cold and lonely country where Anglo-Saxon order and efficiency shape the landscape. Where she is a member of the laboring caste. Whatever success she may have in North America, that feeling of being separated from the essence of herself never leaves her. One of my students writes of a mother who decides to return to Mexico, leaving her grown children behind. "No te quiebres," she tells her son during a tearful farewell, the words summarizing a migrant philosophy: don't break. If this woman was our grandmother, or great-grandmother, the legacy of her journeys, her exploitation, and her resilience can be something as subtle and indelible as the pigment in our skin, the shape of our noses, the color of our eyes. The dark shades we see, or think we see, when we look in the mirror.

ON TELEVISION, IN BARS, AND AT FAMILY BARBECUES, A CERtain kind of "white" person will express their idea of

"Mexicanness," an understanding of one of the "darker," nonwhite tribes of the United States. In Clint Eastwood's movie *The Mule*, a federal agent comes upon a group of tough Latino drug dealers in a Chicago neighborhood and says, "Jesus, it's like the *Star Wars* cantina in there." The Mexican border has become such a powerful image in the United States imagination that the average person equates Latino identity with the border and with a B movie understanding of Mexico as the home of a colorful, alien people with shaved heads who wear serapes. A Peruvian street vendor in New Jersey, a Colombian undergraduate, a Venezuelan janitor, and a Cuban American worker in an Alabama chicken plant are all "Mexicans" to people ignorant of Latin American geography. And "Mexican" itself is a series of stereotypes with echoes of racist attitudes about Native American people. White eyes believe they see the patina of a border or ocean crossing on Latino skin, and they have the sense of us as a conquered people who are allergic to the discipline and the good manners of Anglo-Saxon culture. We sun-darkened people fade into the background of their lives, the supporting players and extras of United States life. Or, like Native "braves" wielding axes in an old Western, we are dangerous when we are on the warpath. You'll see us portrayed as gang members, circling the figurative wagons of white families, in that new U.S. film genre, the cartel movie.

When an immigrant woman arrives in an American city like Los Angeles, the empire gives her an identity that settles over her like a cloak, like the costume of an alien tribe. She can see the power of the empire in the rumble of the patrol cruisers of the many different law enforcement agencies that roam the streets, and in the official emblems and coats of arms on government buildings and sanitation trucks. And yet this new territory represents the possibility of personal liberation, as in the story one of my students tells of her mother, a woman who began working at the age of twelve in Yucatán, running away from her village to work at a tortilla factory; a woman who was forced to marry at age sixteen, and who crossed the United States border at eighteen, to escape the mother who "cut my wings." Like the hero in a Hollywood epic, an immigrant arrives in this country and finds her way. She learns daily lessons about the American people and their odd habits at her new job; and then one night she attends a party in her barrio, and a new friend pushes her into a dance floor of spinning bodies. And the next chapter in her life begins.

THE ESSAYS MY STUDENTS WRITE FOR ME ARE FILLED WITH romantic stories about their parents. They speak of a woman who remembers the seductive sensuality of a young man with his shirt open, or a courtship that began with an encounter on a city bus. From reading their work I've come to see how the United States of our times is a country built on the grunts, the lovemaking, the cursing, the gossip, the heroism, the betrayals, the acts of compassion, the good luck and the bad of Spanish-speaking immigrants. The intimate dramas of their journeys, their twists and turns, are not recorded in multipart television dramas or bestselling fantasy fiction. Instead, a migrant leaves behind a shoebox of letters and photographs stored at the bottom of a closet; or he records key dates and names and addresses on a slip of paper preserved in a wallet for years; or, as one of my students once discovered, he keeps a portrait of a secret "other" family hidden inside an old boot in Georgia. Our collective origin story is a million unfilmed soap operas and a million unproduced *Hamlets*. It's the lovers meeting in a forest of *A Midsummer Night's Dream*, or the strong-willed, independent woman of a Zora Neale Hurston novel.

LIKE "MUTANT," "VULCAN," OR "WOOKIEE," "LATINO" AND "Latinx" and "Hispanic" are the made-up words of storytellers describing a group of people engaged in an adventure. Latino people are brown, Black, white, and Indigenous, and they are European, Asian, and African. Some of us speak excellent Spanish, but many more of us do not. This diverse group of people is joined together by shared roots in the upheavals and the crises set in motion by the building of the United States into a global superpower, and, further back in time, by the Spanish Crown's attempt to build an empire in the Western Hemisphere. This is an obvious truth, one that looms over the daily life of this country, but that is entirely absent from the mass-media discourse about what the United States is. About one in five residents of the United States can trace their roots to Latin American institutions like the encomienda (which granted Spanish conquerors the rights to the labor of Indigenous people) and mestizaje (the new, Eurocentric social order created by "racial" mixing that followed the conquest). All across the United States, there are people whose family histories include events such as the campaigns of ethnic cleansing in Latin America against the Yaqui, Pipil, and other peoples, and the uprisings against U.S.-backed regimes that unfolded in tropical mountains and arid savannas. The wealth and comfort of the people of the United States cannot be separated from this history. If you could take a decades-long, time-lapse film of a typical U.S. suburb, you would see Latino laborers frenetically constructing, demolishing, rebuilding, and remodeling that suburb over and over again; with each day and year of work, they further deepen the presence of Latin American tragedy and ambition in the homes, workplaces, and neighborhoods of the United States.

Over the years a number of my students have shared with me what they have learned about the history of empire and how it has touched their lives. One of their accounts tells of a father haunted by the violence he had seen in El Salvador, in that country's civil war, a conflict fought in the 1970s, '80s, and '90s on mountainsides and on the slopes of volcanoes, and in cities where right-wing death squads and soldiers armed with M16s and machetes mutilated their victims, and where an underground movement spread the idea of social revolution. My student's father had been a rebel fighter, and a relative of his was killed in the government massacre of hundreds of civilians in and around the hamlet of El Mozote. He was an angry and emotionally tortured man, and he eventually took his own life in an apartment in San Francisco, leaving his body for his young daughter to discover. When this student came to my office to discuss the paper in which she described these events, I told her how sorry I was for the loss of her father. You were too young to have lived that, and seen that, I said. Then I told her everything I knew about the revolution and war in El Salvador, and what the violence of that conflict did to the psyche of its people. I wanted to help her see her father's brokenness in the context of his country's brokenness, a horror of "counterinsurgency," napalm, and torture cells, all at the service of "order," class privilege, and the victory of the United States in the "Cold War." I wanted her to understand her father's story, and her own loss and pain, in the context of empire.

Hollywood spends large amounts of money to re-create the horror of empire building and colonialism on-screen. It blows up entire planets, with genocides unfolding on a single page of a movie script. In *Star Wars: The Force Awakens*, the First Order simultaneously destroys five planets of the Republic, and we see an entire civilization wiped out. The stage directions read: "LIKE AN ATOMIC BOMB TEST TIMES A ZILLION . . . FIREBLAST OBLITERATED IT ALL . . . DOZENS OF LANGUAGES EXCLAIMING IN FEAR AND HORROR." The massacres in big sci-fi and fantasy movies have become more realistic and graphic with the passage of film history, as if to try to match the barbarism of real-life events like those that unfolded in Guatemala, El Salvador, and other places in the final decades of the last century.

THE SALVADORAN REVOLUTION IS NOT PART OF THE MAIN-stream public school curriculum in the United States, as I was reminded one day on the subway in Los Angeles. I was scribbling in pencil on the manuscript of the novel I was revising when a young man of about sixteen asked me, with a tinge of sarcasm, if I was doing my "homework." I explained that I was finishing a book about the revolution in El Salvador. He told me his parents were both from El Salvador, but he didn't know anything about a revolution. So I told him some of the stories I'd heard from former rebels when I visited the old battlegrounds of the Salvadoran insurgency. How one campesino transformed a small tractor into a tank, and how the army got so freaked out by one rebel fighter they never managed to capture, they spread the legend that he could transform himself into a tree. I told him about the teenage women who took M16s to fight against an army of rapists. He furrowed his brow with puzzlement, because I had just told him that he and all his relatives were characters in a story with the big-screen sweep, the violence, and the heroism of *The Lord of the Rings*.

In the world of Hollywood fantasy, it's assorted meek peoples from otherworldly realms, most often played by white actors, who fight back and resist and win. "What can men do against such reckless hate?" Théoden, the King of Rohan, asks in *The Lord of the Rings* as the evil army of Saruman threatens to kill the women and children hiding in his fortress. The brave Aragorn tells him he must go to battle. But in real life, the powers that lord over us want us to surrender to their power, and to forget they exist. The empire wants us to believe that empires exist only in fantasies. This is part of its hold over us. The systems that make us subservient peoples are built on the illusion that we are to blame for our own powerlessness. The same media conglomerates that sell us empire fantasy stories have little to say about the real-world truth of imperial violence. And they have nothing to say about the way empires have shaped the intimate worlds of our families. At best, the fantasy factories offer us shallow and stereotypical tales set in a colorful and exotic version of the Global South (with palm trees, prostitutes, and tropical drinks on offer), or in menacing and one-dimensional depictions of the barrios and ghettos of the United States (amid gang members and urban slums). In truth, the forces of empire have conspired to make us into a dumber, hungrier, and more desperate people. Sometimes they have succeeded, and sometimes they have failed; and we are still standing, and breathing, and now we are reading and studying. We are protagonists in a truer, uglier, and more chaotic and interesting story of empire.

I've spent a lifetime trying to sort out my own place in the story of empire and trying to comprehend the power and vulnerability of empires. At first, by listening to the stories my parents told me. And then, as an adult, by visiting Montana battlefields, the site of slave burial grounds in Manhattan, the street corner in Los Angeles where Chinese residents were pulled from their homes to be lynched. Often, this quest has taken on a solitary and spiritual quality. Immigration to the United States ripped my Guatemalan family in two, and my personal memories are an unsettling vapor of chaotic and accidental events. But every time I stand in a spot where the empire's history unfolded, where I can see myself and my family and my countries inside this larger human chronology, the ground beneath my feet grows more solid, somehow.

And that's why, when my children were still small and impressionable, my wife and I packed them into a car and set forth on an expedition southward from Los Angeles. We headed for Tijuana to see the fence the United States government built at the Mexican border, and the spot where its steel sheets and pillars plunge into the sea.

2

WALLS

In the modern United States, the U.S.-Mexico border is our Death Star, the walls surrounding our District 12. If we could rewind the film of real life, in the same way we can scroll backward in the movies we rent or stream, we would see a time when no border barrier existed. We would see open, empty desert lands; a shallow, muddy, and unremarkable river; and a bluff above wetlands facing the Pacific Ocean. In a time long, long ago, in a history faraway, the frontiers of the United States were shifting, imprecise, contested, and unmarked lines that existed only in the imaginations of men.

When you drive from Utah to Idaho you cross the original boundary between the United States and Mexico, the line of the forty-second parallel, an international frontier where no border stations existed. In the spring of 1846, a group of United States emigrants set off from Independence, Missouri, by wagon train, headed for this border and for California, which was then a frontier province of the Republic of Mexico. One of the families hired a teamster named Antonio to guide the oxen pulling their wagons. His last name is not recorded in history, and in the various accounts of the fiasco and tragedy that followed he is described only as twenty-three years old and as "Mexican" or "Spanish."

Independence was also the eastern terminus of the Santa Fe Trail, a nine-hundred-mile route into Mexican territory. There were enough Mexican workers in Independence that year for Francis Parkman, a traveler from Boston, to notice them; he described the mexicano teamsters as subhuman in their appearance. "Thirty or forty dark slavish-looking Spaniards, gazing stupidly from beneath their broad hats." These men had come to Independence, Parkman wrote, "attached to one of the Santa Fe companies," and their wagons were crowded together nearby: it's entirely possible that Antonio was one of those men. In Independence, a Missouri family hired Antonio to work in a California-bound wagon train, but a few hundred miles after they set out, the family changed their minds and decided to head for Oregon instead. Antonio joined another wagon train, led by James Reed and George Donner. Somewhere in the high desert of what is now southwestern Wyoming, Antonio and his new employers entered Mexican territory.

Antonio's employers, and the other white people on the journey, were impatient and eager to reach California, and they took the ill-advised step of following a new shortcut that led them into rocky passes where their wagons became stuck, and where their oxen died crossing salt flats and deserts. They fell hopelessly behind schedule and began to quarrel, and one emigrant stabbed another to death. In so many words, Antonio soon found himself inside an allegory about the dark underside of the United States and the hubris of its people on the western frontier. A seventy-year-old man was deliberately left behind to die because he could no longer walk, and Native tribes stole dozens of the emigrants' oxen and cattle. The Donner Party, as it came to be known, was the very last group of emigrants to reach the Sierra Nevada that year, and soon their progress across the mountain passes was halted by heavy snow and they began to starve. Rather than die with the families huddled in shelters at the bottom of what would later be known as Donner Pass, Antonio joined a small group that tried to cross the snowbound Sierras on foot to reach help on the other side. Within a few days, he died of cold and hunger. The other members of the rescue party cut up his flesh and ate it, and drew strength from Antonio's mortal remains. They cut out his organs too and dried them for future consumption, and in this way they pushed this allegory about the United States and its relationship to the Mexican people to even greater depths of darkness. Luis and Salvador, two Miwok Indians who trekked eastward from the Sacramento Valley to help the stranded emigrants, were killed and also eaten by them.

Had Antonio escaped the purgatory of the Donner Party and lived to complete the journey, he would have discovered a hard truth waiting for him on the other side of the mountains, in the settled part of Alta California. Some months earlier a group of white American migrants had raised a flag adorned with a bear and declared themselves a republic independent of Mexican rule; and then U.S. troops had arrived and claimed California for the United States. Before Antonio lost his life, he had lost a chunk of his country. At about the same time, U.S. troops led by John Charles Frémont (later the first Republican presidential candidate) had massacred about one thousand men, women, and children of the Native Wintu people, an act of barbarism that foreshadowed the horrors of a California genocide to come.

When the United States invaded Mexico, many Americans denounced the actions of their government, including Abraham Lincoln and Henry David Thoreau. But when the fighting was over in 1847, U.S. troops occupied the Mexican provinces of Nuevo México and Alta California, from Santa Fe to San Francisco Bay. In 1848 a U.S. diplomat negotiated the treaty that ended the war, and signed it before the altar to the Virgin of Guadalupe in the town of Guadalupe Hidalgo. Mexico's leaders agreed to surrender half their country's territory to the United States, and a year later commissioners from the two countries met at San Diego to begin to mark out the new frontier. They were to follow the vague description of a border agreed to in Guadalupe Hidalgo by men who had never been to the distant and inhospitable lands through which the new border passed. Surveying in the nineteenth century was a more subjective craft than it is today, and there was much debate and give-and-take between the two teams of commissioners as they studied old Spanish colonial maps and pointed the telescopes in their surveying instruments at various elements of the landscape. Eventually they agreed on the spot where the border should begin. The site was on a bluff overlooking a beach, but this high ground would be needed for a lighthouse, so the commissioners moved the first border marker slightly to the north, on the edge of some wetlands, near the estuary of a river. There was a ranch nearby called Tía Juana, but otherwise no human settlements. The commissioners gathered some stones to mark the spot, and later they ordered a marble obelisk that was shipped in by boat from the eastern United States around Cape Horn.*

* See the opening chapters of *La Gran Línea: Mapping the United States–Mexico Boundary, 1849–1857*, by Paula Rebert.

For many decades, that obelisk was the only physical proof on the Pacific coast that a border existed between the United States and Mexico. Sometimes the Spanish-speaking residents of San Diego, and the occasional English-speaking tourist, trekked down to the beach, and a few carved their initials and names into the monument and wandered back and forth across the border, which was nothing but an imaginary line, stretching from that stone marker into the pale brown mountains to the east.

THE UNITED STATES–MEXICO BORDER WAS BORN OF THE COM-petition between many different powers, over many centuries, to control the vast lands and natural resources of North America, and to dispossess the Native peoples who lived there. The very first barrier built at the spot where the border meets the Pacific Ocean was an iron fence enclosing the original marble obelisk—to protect it from being vandalized. In the 1960s, there were a few strands of barbed wire, and then a chain-link fence of the kind that families put up as an inexpensive way to keep strangers out of their backyards. Today, the imaginary line has evolved into a series of barriers built of steel and concrete, which are, in turn, guarded by a vast army of agents, armed with various instruments of modern technology. In the imagination of certain nativist leaders and thinkers, the border barrier has become, or must become, a "wall" protecting this country from barbarism. The border is a key element in the racial mythology that defines what "Latino" identity is supposed to be. A certain kind of ill-informed white person projects this vision onto their understanding of all the brown-skinned people around them. They see us as a darker people who belong on the other side of the barrier. Walls protect them from cartels and from disease and backwardness. The border has become an element of white identity; it's one more prop in the centuries-long story that has helped pull the heterogenous peoples known as "white" together.

Before "the wall" and the "illegals" there was the "menace" of urban Black people. And before that, there was "the frontier." In the late nineteenth century, the historian Frederick Jackson Turner put forward his "frontier thesis" of American history. In his vision, European-born settlers arrived in a continent that was a blank slate. By taming this unspoiled world, still in a state of nature, white settlers created a unique American democracy and became the optimistic, hardworking, can-do people we know today. Turner's frontier thesis was popular because it captured white America's vision of itself: families homesteading in log cabins, building farms and cities against the challenge of the wild. Native peoples, in Turner's telling, were a part of the natural landscape, a danger lurking inside virgin forests, across vast plains covered with thousands of buffalo; later they would become dioramas in museums of "natural history."

In the U.S. imagination, Latino immigrants are the latest expression of the peril of the frontier, of the dangers that lurk beyond the borders of a "civilization" founded by "white" people. As children, Americans are told the story of the frontier in a series of folktales about "cowboys and Indians," and tales of exploration and "discovery." These stories tend to obscure an essential truth of U.S. history: the pioneer mission was, in large measure, a series of violent acts committed against human beings and the natural world. Every farmer and every wagon train were part of a larger project of collective conquest, individual ambition, and physical intimidation. The settlers and soldiers who marched over the Sierra Nevada and began to destroy the Indigenous cultures of California were part of this project, and so were the emigrants who ate their Mexican teamster and the two Native men who had come to help them.

WHEN THE U.S. GOVERNMENT MILITARIZED LARGE SECTIONS of the border in the 1990s, including urban areas outside Tijuana and El Paso, it forced multitudes of border crossers into the desert. Operation Gatekeeper began south of San Diego with a fence constructed from army surplus steel and morphed into a pharaonic project that included the filling of an entire canyon with about two million cubic yards of hard-packed soil. After the first ten-foot-high wall, and its accompanying seismic sensors and night-vision cameras, the fence underwent several upgrades in the following decades, including the deployment of radar-equipped MQ-9 Reaper drones overhead.

There are now three lines of steel barriers at the bluff where the border overlooks the Pacific Ocean. The obelisk raised by the binational commission of surveyors in 1851 is a foot inside the last barrier. If you are on the U.S. side, you have to peer through a mesh of braided steel to read the inscriptions on the monument's marble skin. When Border Field State Park is open, you can travel to the U.S. half of the "Friendship Circle" that was built around the old obelisk in the 1970s. First Lady Pat Nixon attended the park's dedication, reaching across a few strands of barbed wire to shake hands and touch infants on the Mexican side. Friendship

Circle is now a name that drips with irony, given the Berlin Wall–like barriers that rise there.

There's another park at the spot where Interstate 5 reaches the Canadian border, 1,384 miles away. Peace Arch Historical State Park sits on the forty-ninth parallel, and you can see steel and stone obelisks there that mark the border—and no fences or barriers of any kind. People walk freely inside the park between the Canadian and U.S. sides of the border, in a deliberate statement about how nonthreatening the United States finds its largely "white" neighbor to the north. On a recent visit, I talked to a Royal Canadian Mounted Police officer standing at the edge of a lawn where U.S. and Canadian families were having lunch; I described the "Friendship Park" at the U.S.-Mexico border and the barriers that now divide it. He observed: "That doesn't sound like much of a park, does it?"

In the years since the Friendship Park at the U.S.-Mexico frontier was built, the perceived danger posed by Latino immigrants has grown so much in the U.S. imagination that the border has begun to move inland. There are now Immigration and Customs Enforcement offices deep in the "heartland of America," in places like Salt Lake City, Atlanta, and Omaha. In the modern United States, the border is everywhere.

WHEN I TOOK MY CHILDREN TO SEE THE BORDER FENCE I thought it might cause them to feel a sense of awe. And that maybe, despite their young ages (then twelve, ten, and five years old), they might see the insult of its existence. I was not afraid to take them there, because I had been to Border Field State Park many times and knew it to be a bucolic wetland of brush and sandy soil, favored by birders (for its ospreys and hawks and shorebirds), and heavily surveilled by Border Patrol agents—I carried our U.S. passports with us, just in case. But alas, the park was closed, so we crossed the border, entered Tijuana, and approached the fence from the Mexican side. I have a distinct memory of my children playing on the beach where the border fence dips into the ocean, on the sand near its rusty, steel skin. Fourteen years later, I ask my children about that day; they don't seem to remember much about it. The sun, the sand, the ice cream vendors, and a steel wall and iron pillars driven into the sand: it was just another visit to the beach. My middle son saw the fence in the water and wondered: Can't people just swim around it? Maybe I should have made a little speech, a fatherly "talk" like the one African American parents give their children about encounters with the police. A story about how a people of color are perceived by strangers, and the beliefs others hold about them, and how "the wall" is part of an entire collection of stories about us.

WHEN GLORIA ITZEL MONTIEL VISITS BORDER FIELD STATE Park, she watches from the U.S. side as the ocean laps up against the border wall, which plunges, improbably, a few dozen yards into the surf. "It's such a consolation that the waves and the birds don't care. There's this stupid border there, and the birds jump from one wave to another," she tells me. The border barriers continue away from the beach, rising up and down the hilly landscape like Hadrian's Wall, to the crossing point at San Ysidro that Gloria also visits often. She crossed the border twice as a child, without documents; three decades later, she is a recipient of the U.S.

government status called Deferred Action for Childhood Arrivals (DACA); "deferred" is a legal euphemism that means she remains undocumented, and deportable, in the eyes of the law. Most undocumented people avoid getting close to the border, because even the roads leading there are filled with the agents of the federal bureaucracy that controls their lives. Gloria goes anyway, and sometimes she takes groups of DACA recipients with her. She warns them on the drive down that they'll see a sign on Interstate 5 that says LAST USA EXIT. They enter San Ysidro and proceed to the pedestrian crossing point there. With their pulses racing, they walk into a corridor between ten-foot-tall steel walls to a gate with rotating, one-way turnstile doors that swallow up the border crossers one at a time. Above them, a large sign declares, simply, MEXICO. "This is the passageway," Gloria tells me. "They never felt the ability to return to this place that changed their life." There is barbed wire spooled around the top of the walls of the passageway, and above those walls there is a rusting iron fence that is another fifteen feet tall; the effect is that of an existentialist art installation, a commentary on the cruel bureaucracies and brutal nationalisms that dominate our time.

Gloria tells me that when she first visited these border places she felt "grief." Her past is on the other side of the wall, and it's painful to think that something essential to your being is sealed off from you in this way. Beyond the wall and the border, several hundred miles to the south, there is a village in Guerrero state, outside the town of Iguala. In this town, Gloria was an abanderada in her elementary school, given the honor of carrying the flag and shaking the hand of the president of Mexico when he visited. This was a town with a deeply Indigenous identity, and to this day Gloria wonders why no one in her family speaks an Indigenous language. She first went to the border fence to confront this absence, this rupture in her life, and all the anger directed at her people. Now it's become a habit. After graduating from Harvard, she traveled to San Ysidro almost every week and took her laptop to work on the dissertation for her PhD, typing just paces away from those turnstiles, watching one señora and one paisano after another be swallowed up by the steel teeth of those doors. When I meet her she's thirty-three years old, and as she tells me the story of her life and her relationship with the border, I realize that these repeated border visits are a metaphor for the way she's led her life. Gloria has known she was undocumented for as long as she can remember; as a child the idea that she had been ascribed to a second-class status only fueled her determination. She took each obstacle head-on.

The border and her status gave Gloria a mission with heroic overtones: she was one girl, and then one woman, taking on an empire of wall-builders. Another thinker named Gloria, the late poet and essayist Gloria Anzaldúa, wrote a book called *Borderlands / La Frontera* about the wounds caused by conquest and border-building on the psyche of people known as "Mexican," "Chicano," and "Latino." She imagines a woman traveling to the underworld of the borderlands, taking the deities of the Nahuatl underworld, miktlán, along with her. The journey is the only way to defeat the destructive forces of self-hatred tearing away at her. "Every time she makes 'sense' of something," Anzaldúa writes of her imaginary traveler, "she has to 'cross over,' kicking a hole out of the old boundaries of the self and slipping under or over." She must be willing "to make a hole in the fence and walk across." To know ourselves is to stand before the border that runs through our lives and our history, and to face it, seeing it for all its absurdity and its arbitrariness. A history of inhumanity and prejudice gave birth to the border and its wall, and we can feel the wounds it has inflicted on us. It is a barrier that began as a line that was literally drawn in the sand, by men with telescopes, trying to decide where, exactly, the line should begin.

TODAY, ELLIS ISLAND IS A MONUMENT TO THE IMPOVERISHED Europeans in baggy woolen clothes who migrated to the United States. And you can travel to places like Savannah, Georgia, to visit reconstructed slave quarters, as I did, and see ghostly video representations of enslaved African American people going about their daily labors. But there is no plaque marking the spot in El Paso where bracero laborers from Mexico were sprayed with insecticide in the 1940s, and there is no official monument in the Tijuana River Estuary to the immigrant crossers who made their way through there and transformed the culture of California in the 1980s and '90s. Nor is there an "interpretive center" run by the U.S. Department of the Interior at the many tenement buildings in Los Angeles, New York, Chicago, and San Francisco where Latino immigrants arrived in the first decades of the twenty-first century to begin their North American lives in urban landscapes of flaking lead paint, roaches, and graffitied asphalt.

IN MY STUDENTS' ACCOUNTS OF THEIR FAMILY LIVES, THEY tell of fathers and mothers and grandparents who stand, like people caught in a dream, in a strange plaza, at a freeway exit, in a parking lot. It has taken my students many years of listening, of trying to put together who their mother or father really is, to finally peel away the mystery from the story of their family's crossing. The migrants in their stories carry with them surreal images born of a border crosser's sense of disorientation. When the border became "the wall" and forced migrants to take dangerous paths in the desert, it added an element of horror to telling, as the migrants found themselves the targets of violence fueled by the avarice and the sadism of smuggling networks run by professional criminals. One of my students writes of the emotional distance of an aunt who was raped by a smuggler. "I believe mi tía has created these barriers to prevent someone else from devouring the last piece of herself." Whether we Americans choose to recognize it, or not, these stories have become part of our country's social and psychic landscape. The man who trims the edge of your lawn, or the woman who feeds your baby, may have lived such a story, or know someone close to them who did. Really, no resident of the United States of America has more than two or three degrees of separation from a present-day immigrant crossing story and all its wonders and its dread. Even the forty-fifth president of the United States had undocumented immigrants making his beds for him.

Not too long ago, I traveled to a neighborhood with manicured lawns of crabgrass and an air of humble achievement and stucco order. Here, in Compton, California, middle-class African American and Latino people lived side by side. I went there because one of the houses on the block—the one with a black roof—had been the site of an immigrant hostage drama. About thirty men, women, and children from Guatemala, El Salvador, and Ecuador had been locked in three rooms there and held captive by a pit bull, while their smugglers demanded more money from families who had already paid thousands of dollars. The only inkling the neighbors had that anything was amiss came on the Fourth of July, when a pair of men barbecued on the front lawn, cooking more meat than any two men or any one family could possibly eat. Days later, one of the people trapped inside caught the attention of a neighbor and passed a note on toilet paper asking for help. When the sheriff's department arrived, the smugglers set loose the pit bull; a dozen people ran out and escaped into the alleyways and the nearby thoroughfares of greater Los Angeles, but seventeen were detained and later handed over to immigration authorities, including two Ecuadoran boys, ages seven and nine, who had undertaken the journey alone, in the hope of being reunited with their mother in New York City. A television crew entered the home and captured images that resembled a torture chamber, including a room filled with a horrid stench of feces and another covered with the blood of the pit bull, which had been shot when the sheriff's deputies entered. I interviewed one of the neighbors, an African American woman who had seen the trapped people inside led away, to the sound of handcuffs clanking shut. "When I heard those chains, I shed a tear," she told me. "Thinking of them being hungry and needy. It took me back to what we know, as Black people."

As I sit to write these chapters, I attend a poetry reading by an African American writer. He illustrates his talk with a slide of an infamous image: a diagram illustrating how human beings were crammed and chained together in rows in the hold of a slave ship. Two centuries after the horrors of the Middle Passage, this image still haunts African American people. In our times, the stigma and the legacy of immigrant illegality and the horrors of being smuggled and of crossing deserts shape the way Latino people understand themselves and their histories, even if they are a generation or more removed from their own crossing story. Our collective humiliation is the emotional foundation of the new social class to which most of us belong. We have a grandparent who was a bracero, and even just the label (derived from the Spanish word for "arm") reminds us of the equivalence of Latino people with cheap labor, a status that's tied to our skin color and our present or past immigration status.

MY CHILDREN ARE ALL ADULTS NOW. AND IF I WERE TO TAKE them to see the border fence today, I would most likely speak to them in a professorial tone, the voice of the weary sage they can put up with for about ten minutes. The true insanity of this border wall, I'd say, is that the United States depends on the labor of the people on the other side. It needs and wants immigrants. I might read them that famous passage in *The Grapes of Wrath*, the one in which Steinbeck describes the birth of corporate agriculture in California. Farms became "an industry" run by "batteries of bookkeepers" and "straw bosses," and they imported "slaves" to work their cash crops, Steinbeck wrote: "Chinese, Japanese, Mexicans, Filipinos." This stretch of border was the passageway people followed to become the low-paid workers who helped create an agribusiness empire. The labor of people of color, and especially people of Mexican descent, built the infrastructure that made the booming agriculture of the West possible. Mexicanos cleared land for farming in Texas, built irrigation systems in Arizona and

California. For more than a century, United States growers lobbied Congress and various presidents to allow Mexican workers to cross the border to do this work. Hundreds of thousands, and then millions of us, and of our ancestors, were encouraged and allowed to live and work here—and they were eventually hated and mocked and racialized and transformed into a class of "illegal aliens." The historian Mae Ngai has described this contradictory state of affairs, which lingers to this day, as "imported colonialism."

The tension between dependence on the labor of people of color and immigrants and the hatred and fear directed at them is eternal in United States history. In 1882, slightly more than a decade after Chinese laborers helped build the transcontinental railroad, President Chester A. Arthur signed the Chinese Exclusion Act. Immigrants from southern and eastern Europe provided the labor that built U.S. cities like Chicago and Detroit in the late nineteenth century; and in 1921 and 1924, Congress passed legislation to establish strict immigration quotas from their countries, specifically to protect the "Anglo-Saxon" culture of the United States from the Jews, Italians, Poles, and other European "ethnics." The 1965 law that abolished those quotas tacitly recognized the assimilation of those European "ethnic minorities" into a society dominated by white, Anglo-Saxon people—but it also established limits on immigration from Latin America for the first time. I would tell all this to my children and conclude my speech by describing this fence as the largest instrument of racial engineering ever constructed by the United States of America. The fence was built because California became too brown, and Democrats and Republicans have stretched the fence all the way to Arizona. And once, we had a president who wanted to make it thirty feet tall and two thousand miles long, all because the rest of the country was becoming too brown. And because all three of my children know me too well, they would nod and suppress an eye roll at the obviousness and predictability of me saying all this.

Latino people don't need a lecture to understand the paradox of our place inside United States history. The migrant can sense that the United States is of two minds about her even as she stands on the other side of the border. Like the indentured servants, the Poles, the Germans, and the Chinese people of other centuries, she knows there are factory owners and affluent families on the other side of the fence or the ocean who really want her to make it across, even as the existence of walls, barbed wire, and restrictive immigration laws announce they hate her kind. She knows she has something that is prized on the other side. Her energy, her resourcefulness, the muscle and the persistence and the drive of youth. This is the quality she shares with the indentured servant, the enslaved person, the "Chinaman," the "Paddy." The ability to suffer the extra hour, the determination to stand tall at the end of the workday. Esfuerzo, empeño. A poner garra y corazón. And so she brings herself across.

3

BEGINNINGS

The tale the migrant shares openly, the one she intones to her children on the ride to school, or to her entire family at the dinner table on a holiday evening, is one of youth, optimism, and hope. In this story, the one our mothers and fathers and grandparents will happily repeat, again and again, for the rest of their lives, they will revel in their innocence, their courage, and their resourcefulness. Me fui para Los Angeles, they will say. Or Georgia, or Idaho, or Miami, or Atlanta, or New Jersey. They will tell of their first few encounters with the power of the United States of America: the bus ride, the sea journey, the sterile modernity of the airport terminal, the encounter with an immigration agent, the arrival at that first apartment building in which they found posada. How wonderful and frightening everything seemed in this, the adventure of their lives. In their telling they are like the heroes of fantasy stories, heading off down a road from the Shire, toward Mordor and Mount Doom, toward Oz or District 1, toward California and the Carolinas, and other unknown lands of danger and wonder.

I'VE BEEN LISTENING TO CROSSING AND ARRIVAL STORIES FOR as long as I can remember; I've been a professional listener of these narratives for much of my adult life. Over the years I've heard the shifts from one era of crossings to the next. From the relatively carefree anecdotes of the 1960s and '70s ("I crossed with my cousin's green card," "I was asleep in the back seat next to my sister") to the twenty-first-century horror stories of violation and kidnapping in smuggler safe houses, and the humiliations of prolonged detention in federal facilities. And now my students tell me stories that span both of these eras: about themselves, their parents, and grandparents, and great-grandparents. One of them writes: My father set off from his pueblo in Mexico in 1973, with a guitar, and the dream of meeting the father he had never known. Another: We left Michoacán in an RV, and it wasn't until after we'd arrived, and months had passed and I started school in L.A., that I realized it was a one-way trip. These are origin stories, and even when they take dark turns, they find their way to an ending in a safe, domestic space, to the smells and the light of a kitchen on a bright morning. They are invariably stories about people who find a kind of rebirth when they land here, in the United States, at the age of eighteen, or twenty, or twenty-five. When the muscles in their bellies were still taut, before their eyes went bad and their backs ached day and night. And often they end, as my own family's arrival story does, with a birth.

WHEN MY PARENTS ARRIVED IN LOS ANGELES FROM GUATE-mala, my mother was twenty years old and five months pregnant. Guatemala's last democratically elected government had been overthrown in a U.S.-funded and -organized military coup eight years earlier. A few months later, after I was born at Los Angeles County General Hospital, my father made a conscious attempt to tap into the power of the U.S. empire. He took my mother and me to the Griffith Observatory and pointed a Kodak camera at us, to take one of his first-ever color photographs. The observatory was for my father a symbol of learning, knowledge, and modernity. My mother gave me this image only a few years ago. I was drawn in by its dreamlike qualities, by the strands of faux pearls hanging from her neck, by the way she'd done up her hair, and, above all, by her pose, holding a baby on her lap and looking away from the camera (almost certainly at my father's instruction), into a future she could not yet know. Behind her rises the dome covering the observatory's telescope, a tool for the exploration of the universe. Probably you have a photograph like this somewhere, its full meaning discernible only to you, because only you know the intimate and unwritten truths of the family story behind it.

MY PARENTS SETTLED IN EAST HOLLYWOOD, CALIFORNIA, which was then, and now, a transient corner of a city whose history is itself a story of transience. When the writer Jack Kerouac passed through Los Angeles about fifteen years earlier, he was accompanied by a Mexican American runaway single mom and landed in a flophouse hotel. In his novel *On the Road*, he called Los Angeles "the loneliest and most brutal of American cities." Migrants who come to Los Angeles and other U.S. cities are, more often than not, people who have made a conscious attempt to cut ties to their past. There's an element of recklessness to their actions; invariably, people have tried to discourage them from leaving their homes to come to the United States, but they've left anyway, putting aside the stories of all the things that might go wrong. "You'll go hungry, you'll sleep on the streets, you'll work like a dog." The migrant arrives in a city of runaways reaching for dreams in a landscape of man-made affluence and man-made poverty, where the locals are united in the unfettered pursuit of individualism, and in their collective indifference to the suffering of others. Even the humblest person becomes more cunning in the United States than they would be back home. My parents, as good and earnest as they were when they arrived here, determined in their mission to provide a good home and future for their unborn son, soon learned to grab for the pretty things and people Los Angeles had to offer.

WHEN A MIGRANT ARRIVES IN A NEW CITY AT THE END OF A long journey, it's almost inevitable that he or she or they will land in a place of grime and grit, a community where other poor and unsettled people live. If they are lucky, a room in a home with friends or cousins from the old country awaits them. These friends or cousins will themselves be relatively new to the United States, and they will live in a neighborhood of transience. A Latino "barrio" is born in this way, in boarding rooms, hotel rooms, and overcrowded apartments. Relatives or old friends are squeezed together, living on a street that thumps with music played by strangers, an apartment where the walls emit angry voices. The migrants take all this in and tell themselves: I will not stay here forever, this is not my destiny.

THE NEWCOMER TO THE UNITED STATES CAN'T SEE, AT FIRST, the nation's fraught and violent past. They're too busy trying to earn a living, and when they have a moment to look around, they are bedazzled. Above all, it's the ruthless efficiency of the United States of America that awes the newcomer. They have arrived in the country that invented Taylorism, the science that eliminated "wasted" movement on the factory assembly lines, a concept now applied to the making of hamburgers and cappuccinos. In the Los Angeles of today, and in Houston and Miami and other Sunbelt cities, the recently arrived migrant rides in an old pickup truck on the freeway and sees affluent men and women, alone, in massive sport utility vehicles. These people live in a trance of riches, in urban spaces that are empty of pedestrians and deliberately separated from the immigrant masses. Like their personal vehicles, the servings of food on their plates at restaurants are comically huge. This excess is offensive to the sensibilities of the newcomer. The needy, restless people of the Global South are raised with a more austere worldview. They recycle and reuse. In the poorest corners of their native countries, people live from refuse. But the newcomer soon learns that here, too, in this United States city, there are castes of people who gather discarded objects and transform them into clothing and shelters. United States homelessness is an infinitely lonelier state than poverty in Mexico, Central America, or South America.

The drama of this public brokenness offers a first hint to the newcomer that they have entered a place with its own deep sorrows. Upon their arrival, the new immigrant settles in old segregated neighborhoods, where the great arc of African American history has played out. In the traditionally Black neighborhoods of Los Angeles and New York, deeper in a past invisible to all who live there now, there is a story of Eastern European and Jewish history, and the displaced of Italy, and the British, Ottoman, and Russian empires. Our Spanish-speaking relatives see only the strange and cluttered present: small, tight, and loud spaces of brick and concrete, with iron bars over the windows, and ice cream trucks and families gathered in doorways and on front steps. In these new places, they await what the empire has in store for them.

My parents arrived in Los Angeles, like so many others, leaving behind a country whose history had been shaped by the power of the United States. Guatemala supplies coffee and bananas and cotton and other crops to the Global North—and also mothers to raise children and cook family meals. Imperialism has a certain majesty to it; in fantasy stories that's what you see on the screen and find on the printed page. When I was growing up in East Hollywood, I was too young to appreciate my neighborhood's seedier aspects. I didn't see the sex workers on the streets, or know that the big brick apartment buildings I saw on Hollywood Boulevard housed many people who injected heroin into their veins. Instead, I saw a gleaming metropolis of new roadways and subdivisions, filled with free-living locals and their sunny optimism. The perfection around me was overwhelming. Color television was new. Plastic was new too, and cool, and shaped into bright-colored objects, including radios in the shape of balls and chairs that resembled eggs.

An immigrant hopes to find her way within the rules of the new kingdom in which she finds herself, unaware that with her humility and her labor she is shaping new chapters of that kingdom's history. This happened to my mother. And to your parents or grandparents, or to you, when you were very young.

IN THE ACCOUNTS OF SOCIAL SCIENTISTS, AN IMMIGRANT community is created by people who make decisions as if they were carrying small charts and pie graphs in their heads. People migrate because wages are higher in "el norte," the schools better, the streets safer. But this portrait robs the immigrant of her gusto for life, of the grand troublemaker inside him, her, them. El pícaro, los sinvergüenzas, la chingona. The great, unspoken truth of the birth of the Latino barrios that grew across the United States in the twentieth and early twenty-first centuries is that their creation was, in no small measure, an event shaped by the hormonal passions and the impatience of youth. By the willfulness and stubbornness of teenagers and young adults, who collectively brought new Latinx families, and new communities into being with their libidos and their fearlessness. The Latino barrios of this country were born of family conflict and tragedy and misunderstandings and dysfunction. Everyone who's ever listened to an immigrant when their tongue is loosened knows this. The heroes in our family histories carry traumas, and they are prideful, and there's not a little irrationality to their behavior. Uncertainty and chance are key elements of the migratory equation. As one of my students writes, quoting her parents about their journey to the United States: "We arrived here like dandelion seeds, floating through the air, reaching firm ground by the blessing of God."

The people now called "Latino" carry the collective memory of the arrival of a young and bold migrant. It's a story that can live on, silently and secretly, in a mood, a disposition, passed down from one generation to the next. In the work of one of my students, an immigrant keeps a photograph of his village birthplace in El Salvador attached with magnets to the steel surface of a refrigerator in a United States suburb. To his American-born daughter, the juxtaposition of two contrasting scenes of domesticity is jarring; she sees the spartan adobe structure and dirt floors in the old photograph, while standing in the air-conditioned, carpeted American space in which she was raised. In that moment she thinks of the younger, thinner iteration of her father, and she feels the success and tragedy of him, and the scars poverty and migration left on him, and she thinks of all the years she's lived inside the intimate wound of his loneliness and his ambition.

To have young parents is a blessing and a curse. The children of young parents witness the hurricane of their parents' passions crashing into the responsibility of family and work. My students tell stories of their parents' youthful energy, their mistakes. They describe the bitterness and frustration their parents feel when they slowly become aware this country wants to keep them small and low; and they have seen their parents rebel against this realization with acts of stubbornness, brilliance, and, sometimes, self-destruction. Their parents go to AA and they pray, and sometimes one of them disappears completely, across the border or borders, and then he returns, months or years later, suddenly full of hope, plotting his next move.

THE SANITIZED VERSION OF MY PARENTS' FIRST DAYS IN THE United States, the one I've told in the pages of my hometown newspaper and assorted other publications, goes something like this: After a night or two in an East Hollywood apartment with Ruby, my father's old neighbor from Guatemala, my parents found a one-room apartment of their own nearby, in a tenement building on a street called Madison Avenue. A few hundred feet away, there was a public library whose construction was funded by Andrew Carnegie, the steel tycoon. My father found a self-study English course there that he brought home. He enrolled in adult-school classes, too, and took jobs as a busboy and as a parking-lot valet and in the hotel business, and my mother got clerical jobs. And eventually they both got their U.S. citizenship and sent their only son to college.

The unsanitized version of this story is messy, and telling it publicly causes unpleasantness in my family. My parents were attractive people who had conceived a child out of wedlock in Guatemala City in the back of a delivery van, no less. (There are two kinds of mothers: those who will dish on the dirty details of your conception, and those who will not. My mother is in the former category.) My father married my mother in an act of responsibility that was motivated, in part, by the painful separation of his own parents when he was very young. Once he was in Los Angeles, however, he let his eyes drift toward many of the beautiful woman who passed in his path. And since it was Los Angeles in the 1960s and '70s, there were so, so many. My mother eventually brought home a new lover too. While my parents were married, and in the years and decades that followed their divorce and their other marriages and divorces after that one, they hurled accusations of infidelity at each other. I forgive them for everything, because they were young and attractive and set free from the strictures of the prying relatives and neighbors of pious Guatemala into a city of miniskirts and men with long sideburns and loosened shirt buttons who preened and oozed desire. Life wasn't all work and sacrifice. I'm glad they enjoyed the beautiful things and people California had to offer. And I'm grateful they allowed themselves to focus their attentions on raising me as much as they did.

IN MY EARLIEST CHILDHOOD MEMORIES, I AM A FLUENT EN-glish speaker who lives inside a home where Spanish is the principal language. These memories unfold in the place my parents lived next, a one-bedroom duplex in another corner of East Hollywood, on a street called Harold Way. I slept in a bed in the same room as my parents and I was conscious of the fact that I was growing inside the warmth of the yellow light that streamed through the windows, and this knowledge filled me with a sense of destiny and hope.

All children are born guileless. But I look back now at the first years of my life, and I see an especially deep well of innocence. My parents carved out this space of safety with their love and optimism, with constantly repeated messages that I was a special child and that I lived in a country that would allow me to shape the future to my will. My mother danced with me and told me stories of her love affair with my father, and in this way she gave me self-love and made me strong for a lifetime of struggle. Not every immigrant kid grows up this way, but many do. My parents did not tell me that I lived in a city that was divided into Black and white, Jew and gentile, Mexican and non-

Mexican, favored and excluded. They protected me from what they knew of these truths. As young outsiders themselves, they could not possibly have known how deeply ethnic and racial hatred had shaped the landscape of asphalt, concrete, palm trees, and stucco that surrounded them, and how it lingered, even, in the air scented by the blossoms of the aging orange trees around us.

4.

CITIES

My hometown is located on a flat coastal plain once covered in brush, and intersected by rivers and creeks where pure water has bubbled up from springs since the dawn of the Pleistocene. As a settled, human place, it has belonged to the Tongva and to three different empires. Once it was a rural outpost of the Spanish Crown, and then a Mexican pueblo until it was taken by the United States in a war of conquest and became what it is today: the newest and last megalopolis built in the westward march of Western civilization across the Western Hemisphere. From its first days, Los Angeles was a place where the racial categories of empires mattered, and where people struggled to shake off the markings and the namings of race.

The forty-four original settlers of Los Angeles carried with them the racial designations of New Spain, labels that appeared in the town's first census, in 1781: "mulato," "mestizo," "indio," "negro," and "español." In the next count, nine years later, many of these first Angelenos had become lighter. Pablo Rodriguez, an "indio" in 1781, became a "coyote" (three-quarters Indian, one-quarter European) in the 1790 census; José Moreno went from "mulato" to "mestizo," and José Navarro from "mestizo" to "español." Within a generation, this ethnically fluid group of people, assembled mostly from the lower castes of New Spain, shook off those old categories altogether and gave themselves a rebirth into a new ethnic identity, Californio.

Pío Pico, born in 1801 and the most famous Californio of his time, was an Afro-Español (today we'd say he "presents as Black") whose father spoke the Indigenous language Tongva and who married a fair-skinned woman from a well-off Los Angeles family. Before the U.S. conquest, Pío Pico rose to become a member of the California elite (he was the last Mexican governor of California), and he epitomized the aspirations of Californios as an ethnic group; the idea that they had somehow transcended the lower castes of New Spain and become "people of reason." In photographs of the day, he wears the silk cravat and embroidered vest of the provincial aristocrat he aspired to be. After the United States conquered California, Pico sold ranchlands to build what he hoped would be the most glamorous hotel in the heart of the American city Los Angeles was destined to become. Pío Pico and his fellow Californios no longer carried the stigma of indigeneity and Blackness, but after the U.S. takeover the "white" newcomers who came to dominate the politics of California introduced new race ideas and race-centered laws. The Californios were swallowed up by waves of migrants from the midwestern, eastern, and southern United States, and by the arrival of immigrants from Mexico, and by a new racial term, "Mexican." When spoken by "white" people, the English translation of "mexicano" carried new social meanings. In the English-speaking Southwest, "Mexican" became the name of a lower social caste, and a slur. In 1930, "Mexican" was a racial category in the U.S. census for the first and only time, at about the same time that the United States was deporting between four hundred thousand and two million people in the "Mexican Repatriation," as many as half of whom were U.S. citizens.

When I was born in Los Angeles, nearly two centuries after the city's founding, a hospital official or nurse listed my parents as "Caucasian" on the birth certificate issued by Los Angeles County and the State of California. Like the first settlers of Los Angeles, my parents had been officially lightened by their journey to California. For my father, with his mestizo coloring, being labeled Caucasian was a physical whitening; for my mother, who is fair-skinned, it was a social lightening, a categorization that made her one with European Americans, despite her nonexistent English and the very brown Mayan father she had left behind in Guatemala. Thanks to the millions of Latin American immigrants who followed them in the 1980s, the label "Caucasian" never stuck to my parents. In the same way that the Californios became "Mexicans," Latin American immigrants of my parents' generation could not shake their alien identity. In the late twentieth century, immigration from Latin America was increasingly criminalized, and the Border Patrol grew severalfold, its agents roaming cities like Los Angeles and Phoenix and Denver to hunt down members of a new juridical category: "illegal alien." This term, which has roots in laws that were explicitly aimed at shaping the racial and ethnic look of the United States, has become, in everyday usage, a racial category. Illegal alien and its synonyms ("illegals," especially), are used freely in the United States, applied in insults, in polite conversation, and in television punditry, where millions of people are routinely mocked and racialized. Some thirty years after the birth of their son and their naturalization ceremony as U.S. citizens, my parents would live to hear their child rechristened with a new slur: "anchor baby."

Race labels and insults aim to "put us in our place." Where is this "place" and what does it look like and what does it mean to be put there? Unhappiness and stigma can define an "ethnic" place, or a place "of color," as I've seen in the writing of my "white" students who tackle the subject of their ancestors' fraught relationship with race, ethnicity, and the idea of white and Black. One tells me of her grandfather turning away from his Portuguese heritage in California because of the powerful memories of humiliation he suffered as an olive-skinned Iberian immigrant in the United States of his youth, and the shock and sting of the day he worked in the sun too long and was confused for a Black man; having momentarily entered a place of Blackness, he sought the protection of abstract, irrefutable whiteness for the rest of his life.

For as long as the idea of race and ethnic identities have existed, people have tried to move back and forth across the geographical, institutional, and emotional boundaries of those identities. In California history, we can read of a Jewish man being excluded from the Los Angeles Country Club in one era, and then accepted by the gentiles in another. In her *Harvard Law Review* article "Whiteness as Property," Cheryl I. Harris tells the story of her Black grandmother, a very fair-skinned woman who passed as white in her Chicago workplace, returning every day to her home and family in an African American community. Eventually, her guilt after a lifetime of passing and traveling back and forth across the city's racial boundaries led her to embrace the Civil Rights Movement; in the same essay Harris tells of "passing" Black people who left the South in the era of Jim Crow to live in northern cities as white people, and whose Black families never heard from them again.*

In the modern American city, race and ethnic identities are more confused than ever, and often people see us in the costume of an identity that doesn't fit us. Or they study us, allowing their gaze to fix on us too long (something that happens quite often to my students who are from mixed "Asian-white" families) because they don't know where to "place" us. Sometimes they completely, and disastrously, mis-place us.

One day circa 2010, I was dressed in the costume of American middle-class leisure (an untucked Oxford shirt, blue jeans, tennis shoes), when I went to see my oldest son, then a teenager, play in a soccer game at a suburban park. I was standing on the sideline, alongside a very multicultural and very L.A. set of parents (white, Asian, Latino) when a young white child of about six approached me, holding a dollar bill. "Can I have an ice cream?" he asked. I had never seen this boy before. I scanned the people around me in confusion; about ten yards away, separated from me by at

---

* Latino is the most open-ended and loosely defined of the "nonwhite" categories in the United States. As such, it can feel like the transit lounge of American identities, one where people come and go with relative ease. Like the writer H. G. Carrillo, an African American man from Detroit who assumed a Cuban American identity; or like countless men and women who've married into Latino families and adopted their Spanish surnames in their professional lives; or like actors such as Oscar Isaac (Hernández Estrada), who is Guatemalan and Cuban and whose roles include an Armenian student, an Egyptian pharaoh, and a French painter.

least two other parents, I saw a street vendor and his ice cream cart. This boy had scanned the faces of the adults on the sideline and deduced that the immigrant vendor and I were working together. The boy had, in his own way, put me in my "place." I could say nothing in response, other than: "You see that man over there, standing behind the cart? He's the one selling the ice cream." (My wife remembers that I had tears in my eyes.) Obviously you can't accuse a six-year-old boy of being a racist. He was merely responding to the racial and ethnic patterns he saw in the city in which he lived: street vendors in greater Los Angeles tend to be people with my coloring and features. Being an observant six-year-old, he was slowly developing his own sense of the colorized geography of the city in which he lives.

WHEN MY PARENTS ARRIVED IN LOS ANGELES, THE CITY'S geography had been shaped for decades by the race- and ethnocentric project of assorted property developers, real estate agents, and city officials. In a 1939 map produced by the Federal Home Loan Bank, Los Angeles is divided into four, color-coded zones: green and blue, "Grade One" and "Grade Two," were the most desirable, and race restrictions were enforced there to keep those neighborhoods white. Yellow and red were "Grade Three" and "Grade Four," neighborhoods that were home to the groups at the bottom of the city's hierarchy, including Blacks, Mexicans, and poorer white people of varied "ethnic" groups, including Jews and Eastern Europeans. The thin lines and pale primary colors of this map give it an ancient aura; it resembles those drawings you see in the endpapers of fantasy novels, the ones that describe the boundaries of imaginary kingdoms and territories, with dragons swimming in the surrounding seas.

As a child, I lived in a district of the city that was colored yellow on this map. Grade Three. Up the steep hill of Western Avenue there was a blue neighborhood across Franklin Avenue, and higher up, the green Grade One neighborhoods of the Los Feliz mansions where my childhood friends and I never ventured. The modern-day, segregated order of United States cities, with their divisions of race and class, was born in the threat of violence represented by police departments and lynch mobs, and by the corruption and prejudice practiced for decades in city planning departments. Go to any American metropolis and study its history, and you'll find people of color living in the neighborhoods where free Black communities existed during the years of slavery, or in communities that were born in the mid-twentieth century as the labor camps of Mexican, Filipino, and Japanese migrants. You'll learn how people of color were confined to certain spaces, by law, and how segregation was given a new and extended life in the twentieth century by a host of government policies and business practices, including the discriminatory lending policies and the mass expulsions of "urban renewal." As Harris argues in "Whiteness as Property," the United States transformed the myth of white identity into a social commodity and granted those who possessed it a power similar to that possessed in the law by the owners of property. In his book *The Possessive Investment in Whiteness*, the scholar George Lipsitz describes how government and business policies created exclusively white spaces, while government and business channeled public and private resources away from nonwhite people; in this fashion, the cash value of white identity increased, and the benefits of past discrimination have been passed down like property to new generations.

AS CHILDREN WE LISTEN TO THE ADULTS AROUND US MAKE observations about skin color and where it places us; we sense their anxiety when we travel with them beyond the safety and familiarity of our own neighborhoods. Eventually we come to the realization that the outside world sees our laboring parents, our undisciplined classmates, and our tattooed cousins as social menaces. This knowledge creates a storm of confusion and frustration within us, because at school and on television we are fed a steady diet of platitudes about the United States being the land of equality and justice.

One of my students describes the bullying he experienced when he traveled from one end of his native metropolis to another, so that he could attend school "on the other side" of its invisible divide. His imagination transformed his anxiety and anger about this daily journey into a fantasy story in which he became an anime hero battling evil. "The world was my archnemesis like how Goku was Vegeta's, or Han Solo was Boba Fett's, or Magneto was Professor Xavier's, or Naruto was Sasuke's." Today, the young and the free-spirited and the hormonal can still feel the way segregation and inequality cage them in and limit their horizons. They realize that, as modern as the world has become, the ancient thinking of old empires is alive all around them.

The geography of the cities of the United States is an assault on our bodies and our free will. We can feel the empire's inner borders in the rutted surfaces of the roads of our neighborhoods, the crumbling bus benches, the rusting wire fences. "Los cholos had a house across the street that was completely boarded up. No light entered the house," one of my students writes. "It looked like a wooden dungeon that kept prisoners locked up for an eternity." The student who wrote those words adds, bitterly, a description of his hometown as "a shitty little city that was infested with rodents and stray dogs." Many of my students write of the dangers they face when they venture beyond the boundaries where they're "supposed to be." Police patrol the city's invisible divides and carry deadly weapons as they do so. A student of Afro-Dominican-Mexican heritage describes sitting down with his mother in their kitchen in Queens, to receive "the talk," the day after Eric Garner, a Black man, was killed by a police officer in New York. "My mother is a headstrong, stubborn woman," my student writes. "I had never seen her so serious, yet so worried, in my entire life." She spoke words meant to protect him as he traveled about the patrolled spaces of New York, teaching him to submit to the power of the forces of order, so that he could live to see another day.

THE PHYSICAL INSULT OF NORTH AMERICAN URBAN GEOGRA-phy, and its race, ethnic, and class segregation, helped give rise to the culture of the homeboy, homegirl, and gang member. And to the "cholo," a word that can now be found in most dictionaries of American English, but that has origins in the caste terminology of colonial Spanish America. A cholo was a mixed-race person of either Indigenous or Afro-Indigenous ancestry, and in Mexico it eventually became synonymous with the socially and culturally marginal. There are many cholos and gang members in my students' writing. One tells of a cholo cousin killed in a shooting, and describes the relationship he and his gang had with her mother. "He was your brother, more than a cousin. So were all the other gangster bodyguards you had back in the day. You had the full force of F-Troop to protect you, even if you swore you were never a chola. Your bamboo gold hoops and NYX nutmeg lip liner could have fooled me into thinking you were one."

Before there were "cholos" and "cholas," there were "pachucos." In the middle of the twentieth century, the Mexican writer Octavio Paz visited Los Angeles and described what he saw as the sad, tragic performance of pachuco culture, with its distinctive fashion statement, the zoot suit. The pachuco, Paz wrote, was "an impassive and sinister clown whose purpose is to cause terror instead of laughter." To Paz, the alienated Mexican American young man of Los Angeles was a person who had lost his Mexican identity but did not fit in the United States; his violent acts transformed him into "his true self . . . a pariah, a man who belongs nowhere." This is one of the many things that Paz got wrong about Latino people in the United States. In fact, the pachuco and the pachuca, the cholo and the chola and the cholx, were in the past and remain in the present very much aware of where they belong. The barrio is their everything, a piece of the city worth fighting for. They hold on to their sense of belonging to a community of brown-skinned, handsome, and proud people. Read Luis J. Rodriguez's memoir *Always Running*, and you'll feel the deep sense of brotherly and sisterly and familial love that underpinned the author's life in his barrio, despite the shootings, beatings, and arrests that defined his gang life to the outside world.

The defiance of the cholo or gang member is born from feeling, deep in their beings, the violence and debasement upon which segregation and racism are built. Their tensed forearms and temples are the muscle memory of a conflict whose beginning is lost deep in a forgotten history, the original sin of enslavement and conquest from which the racial hierarchies of the present were created. Once upon a time, the armies that defended their people were defeated by soldiers armed with muskets and cannons; and today the enmities of those ancient battles live on in cities where police are armed with Berettas, Glocks, and Smith & Wessons, and where an "interior colonialism" reigns.

Today, scholars have begun to show the link between the ethnic prejudice and violence of the Manifest Destiny era of U.S. history and the growth of the carceral-corporate state in our times. In Kelly Lytle Hernández's *City of Inmates*, we see how greater Los Angeles, a metropolis that now incarcerates more people than any other city in the United States (in jails, prisons, youth camps, immigration detention, etc.), first locked up large numbers of Native peoples in the nineteenth century in a campaign to create a captive labor force for public and private construction projects. In the late twentieth century, technology began to expose the ugliness of Los Angeles's colonial policing mentality. In 1991, a year before Los Angeles exploded in rioting, an early form of text messaging caught the LAPD's racist attitudes about Black and Latino people: "Batten down the hatches, several thousand Zulus approaching from the north . . . Nothing but wetbacks no speaky English and ugly." Over the years, I've had many students tell me, with pride, "I'm from South Central Los Angeles," and in that simple statement they are telling a story about two kinds of people, Black and Latino, who live alongside each other in a kind of internal colony, perpetually at war with the city around it, patrolled by officers from four different LAPD divisions, the singed walls and ruins of battles past still visible in the landscape.

MY LATINX STUDENTS ARE ANGERED BY THE RACE AND CLASS order that subjugates them. They tell stories of encounters with police, traffic stops that seem designed to teach them a lesson about their "place" in their hometowns and in their country. Unable to overthrow this order, they describe friends and relatives who often turn on one another, because they need to keep fighting—someone, anyone—to prove to outsiders and to themselves that they have not been defeated, subjugated, and emasculated.

One of my students is a U.S. Marine veteran. He remembers his youth in a Latino barrio and the stupid macho confrontation that escalated into an armed encounter not long before his first overseas deployment. "We come from a line of peleoneros," my student writes of his family. People who like to fight. An altercation ensues at a party over the flimsiest excuse possible—the football jerseys two of the partygoers are wearing. Punches are thrown; promises of revenge follow. My student goes "on point" at the edge of the party, awaiting a retaliatory ambush, and sure enough a guy shows up with "a jet-black subcompact pistol he was looking to unload." My student intervenes to prevent further bloodshed. A few months later he is shipped off to Iraq, where he routinely witnesses the harassment of the locals for "driving while Iraqi." He and his fellow soldiers call themselves "the Dark Side," and his platoon commander urges him to commit war crimes. "I felt the pressure to step up my craziness when I was around him, plus he was raza, so I had to back him up." The irrational, violent behavior deemed a felony in his Santa Ana, California, barrio could make my student a patriotic "American hero" when he was shipped overseas.

IN OTHER TIMES, IN OTHER CONTEXTS, THE VIOLENCE OF GHETtos, barrios, and "slums" has been socially acceptable and celebrated. Most present-day governments can trace their roots to movements whose ranks included urban criminals and social outcasts. During the early days of the French Revolution, the residents of the poor districts of Paris stormed the Bastille prison and spit upon, kicked, and killed the disarmed prison guards and officials; a few psychopaths in their ranks decapitated people with pocketknives and paraded about the city with their victims' severed heads on pikes. Bastille Day is now a national holiday in France because the violence of the criminal elements of Paris helped propel a political revolution that culminated in the birth of French democracy. The ideals of that revolution were summarized in one of the great documents of Enlightenment thinking: the Declaration of the Rights of Man and of the Citizen.

The angry posture of the barrio tough guy is his own declaration of human worth. His worldview is a daily battle against the self-hate born of difficult childhoods and family dysfunction. He can sense that outsiders are repelled by his indelible brownness, and that powerful forces are trying to humiliate and belittle him and his loved ones. A thin line separates his "irrational" behavior from the forces that create "civilization." All he needs is a Bastille to storm, and a new Enlightenment to give voice to his humanity, and to perhaps liberate him, once and for all.

THOSE WHO STAY IN THE BARRIO BUILD THINGS AND ROOT themselves to its plots of land. They create their settledness and their own peace of mind; adapting to the unequal urban geography, they fight for their humble piece of the city. Many of my students have told me how much they love their barrios, and how they think of these neighborhoods as places of wisdom, love, and suffering. "People have always had hopes in this little town of mine," one writes. They describe the vast cast of characters in their communities. A man who is a fixture on Pacific Boulevard, the main drag of the Los Angeles suburb of Huntington Park, wears "a white sombrero, black button vest with a white shirt, cowboy boots, and his short hair slicked in a small ponytail." They find ways to dance around the boundaries in their lives, and make light of them, and sometimes to cross them. One enters a tattoo parlor where she is inked with an image of the Virgin of Guadalupe with an LGBTQ flag. This is a bold thing for a Mexican daughter to do, so for a few days she hides said ink with a long-sleeve shirt, lest her mother see it, until the day comes when she allows her rainbow-Virgin to breathe the open air of the barrio, and to force all of her neighbors and friends and relatives to deal with it, and with her and her rebellious sexuality.

ONE OF MY STUDENTS DESCRIBES THE WATER TOWER AT THE center of the agricultural town where he grew up, and the four quadrants that divided the town by ethnicity and class, and the nicknames the locals assigned to those neighborhoods: "Fresa City," for instance, for the whitest of the neighborhoods, "fresa" being a Mexican word for strawberries that is also slang for the affluent and pampered. "Walking around that part of town I felt like I always had to dress a certain way and not talk Spanish unless I wanted people to mad-dog me or call the cops because I'm walking the streets and looking suspicious." When his family moves to Fresa City they antagonize their white neighbors by playing cumbias loudly or parking their taco truck in the driveway.

Another student, who is Vietnamese American, describes the overlapping Asian and Latino geographies in a community where people of both ethnicities live in a marginal corner of Southern California's sprawl. This cohabitation is repeated inside the neighborhood grocery stores, with Vietnamese phở bouillon on offer on one aisle and bottles of Mexican mole sauce on the next. She describes the spicy enchantments offered to her by her Latina friends, including the Mexican American girl at her school who supplemented her family's income by selling "Vero Mango chili lollipops, Salsagheti, Pulparindo, Flamin' Hot Cheetos with limón, Xxtra Flamin' Hot Cheetos, Takis." Her young Latina friend set herself up on the school grounds like a street vendor, complete with a bottle of lime juice and "Valentina hot sauce" for her customers to sprinkle on their purchases. My Vietnamese student writes of these delights with the affection a Spanish-speaker would call cariño; they flavored and warmed her life inside a neighborhood that was a lesser place to outsiders.

The Orange County neighborhood where my student lives is famous as Little Saigon, but about one-quarter of the residents there are Hispanic and another quarter are white, according to the census. This is a truth about American cities we are not taught in our textbooks: most urban immigrant enclaves in United States history, including most Latino barrios, are places where people of many different nationalities and ethnicities encounter one another.* The Swedish "ghetto" of Chicago in the 1930s was only one-quarter Swedish, and one of the oldest Mexican American street gangs in that city was originally made up of Poles. Paterson, New Jersey, is the site of an annual Dominican pride parade and famous as a center of the Dominican diaspora in the United States (Junot Díaz set much of his landmark novel, *Oscar Wao*, there). But Paterson is one-quarter Dominican; it also hosts a Little Lima of Peruvian homes and businesses, as well as a large African American community. In Orange County, Chicago, and Paterson, clusters of outsider and immigrant peoples live together in historic "Grade Three" and "Grade Four" neighborhoods, places where the journeys of migrants of different ethnicities overlap and intersect.

In our schools and colleges, we are taught a version of our national history in which each ethnic and racial group lives in its own narrative channel, following the logic of its own traditions and suffering. In bookstores and libraries, the various ethnic histories of the United States are shelved separately. Writing history one ethnic or racial channel at a time was, and is, a necessary corrective to the erasures of the stories and contributions of people of color. But when

* Among the scholars who have explored this is George J. Sánchez, in his book *Boyle Heights: How a Los Angeles Neighborhood Became the Future of American Democracy*.

we tell the story of a community that way, we can miss all sorts of human-created complexity; it's like listening to a symphony in which each musician enters the concert hall and plays the entirety of their contribution to the work separately and then leaves the stage for the next musician to play their part. What emerges is something less beautiful and less compelling than the act of cooperation and coordination you can hear when all the musicians perform onstage together.

WHENEVER I STOP TO THINK ABOUT "LATINO" HISTORY, OR TO teach it, I find the stories of other peoples next to ours. Like my Vietnamese student, who titled the story she wrote for me "Chicano Chinita." Or the Chinese American young woman who described her parents' anger when she brought home a Salvadoran boyfriend. When I visit the Latino evangelical church that meets in a building on Martin Luther King Jr. Boulevard in Los Angeles, I discover the property is owned by a Baptist congregation; the Baptists are African Americans, and they conduct services there too, while also renting to the evangelicals, who are mostly immigrants from Central America. I see Hebrew writing over the doorway and with a quick bit of research I discover the building was constructed in the 1920s (when King Boulevard was known as Santa Barbara Avenue) by members of a religious community founded by Ashkenazi Jews, most of whom had emigrated from the island of Rhodes when it was still part of the Ottoman Empire. On Rhodes they endured the arrests and the beatings provoked by the blood libels spun against them by Ottoman Christians, and in Los Angeles they lived, for a time, alongside Black people who had fled the lynchings and the humiliations of the empire called Jim Crow.

The East Hollywood neighborhood where my family settled is today called Little Armenia. But it could just as easily be called Thai Town, or Historic Filipinotown, which are the names city officials have given to two adjacent neighborhoods—either of which could also be called Little Centroamérica. In East Hollywood, my Guatemalan immigrant family lived alongside white people who were on the margins of whiteness. My school friends were of Armenian, Serbian, and Slovak descent; and a poor white kid from Arkansas whose father had been killed in Vietnam. They had parents and grandparents who had roots in the Balkan former provinces of the Ottoman Empire, and in the polyglot Austro-Hungarian Empire. I had friends whose parents were born in the Philippines when it was still a United States colony. There were mexicanos, too, and African Americans, like my godfather Booker Wade, who had come to Los Angeles to escape the racial segregation of Memphis, Tennessee.

In sum, I grew up in a United States city surrounded by people with legacies of violence and empire in their pasts, histories that spanned the globe. We were gathered together in our Grade Three neighborhood, in lesser flatlands beneath the trendy and tony Hollywood Hills and the Sunset Strip. With each passing year, our lives became ever more intermingled with the city's history of violence. A chunk of Los Angeles burned to the ground when I was two years old, the first fires lit in a community called Watts, which is colored red, the lowest grade, in that old developers' map. Twenty years earlier the city witnessed the "Zoot Suit Riots," a pogrom against Mexican American pachucos that unfolded on downtown streets lined with some of the nation's first big movie palaces. A short walk to the north, kitty-corner from the spot where my future wife and I later obtained our marriage license, Chinese residents of the city were lynched at a corral in 1871; many other people were hanged by vigilantes and mobs at this spot too, including a French immigrant who murdered one of his Native American employees, and whose final words included one last ethnic insult: "I am hung by a set of Germans and Jews because I am a Frenchman!"

This is the world my libidinous, attractive, daydreaming parents entered. And the world into which I was born. A complicated and cruel space of perceived and constructed differences of race, overlying deep divisions of class. A city where newly arrived immigrants and migrants could plot a future of security and abundance—and where at least one neighbor of ours was an unapologetic and ambitious racist.

My white-supremacist neighbor was a man of forty who I never met, but whose story I know from my later reading of United States history. He had lived most of his life in transient and hard places, as many newly arrived migrants do. It could be said my neighbor was a kind of "white" outsider within the borders of the American cities in which he lived. James Earl Ray was obsessed with whiteness. Race is a way to imagine one's superiority to others and is a strategy for dealing with hurt, and both these things were true of my neighbor and his ideas about being white. He had been born in Alton, Illinois (two years later and one mile away from the future jazz great Miles Davis), but his life soon took him, as a child and as a young adult, from one rough corner of the Midwest to another.

When this man moved in next to us in Los Angeles in

1967, he had been denied the privileges of true, pampered "whiteness" for his entire life. Perhaps for this reason, he was obsessed with race, with its seemingly immutable categories, its "truths" about different people and their intelligence and their behavior, and the divine order that they be separated. Even though he was never formally educated, he studied race and talked incessantly about it. My neighbor was plotting an act of murder that would elevate the white race and assure its supremacy into a proud and angry future.

On the other side of the fence at the back of his apartment building, my family lived in a duplex apartment. In this peaceful and quiet corner of an angry and crowded city, I was learning my *ABC*s.

5

RACE

For my white-supremacist neighbor, James Earl Ray, darkness was the threat he saw nearly every place he lived. Blacks, Mexicans, Asians, Jews. He lived one hundred feet from us, our kitchen window facing his bedroom window, and it's entirely possible that the scent of my mother's pot of black beans cooking reached him on a late spring morning, or a summer afternoon. The scent of onions and garlic and salt, drifting over the jade plants in our backyard, wafting through his open back window.

White means the absence of color. If you're white, it's supposed to mean you no longer carry the suffering of people of color. You are free of the melas, or blackness, of melanin and melancholy. You are outside the hurt of history. When I study the life of James Earl Ray and his attempts to create an identity for himself, I see a longing to wrap himself in the exalted cloak of whiteness, and the many fictions of whiteness. White was his superiority, his power in a world that, at various times, made him feel small, caged, and hunted.

His family had a long history of wandering from one

poor corner of the Midwest to another. The men in his family drank too much, and the Rays changed their names several times because his father was wanted for forging checks and other crimes. His great-grandmother was an Irish immigrant, but as far as I can tell Ray never practiced or celebrated any of the traditions of the Irish; most of his family, historians would later determine, was of British descent. Instead, he sought power in the abstraction of "white," following the example of his virulently racist, ex-convict father. After committing his own crimes, the younger Ray, as an adult inside the Missouri prison system, read and studied the writing of white supremacists, and he considered moving to the white-ruled and white-supremacist nation of Rhodesia, now known as Zimbabwe.

In the various accounts of his family's life that were penned after he murdered Martin Luther King Jr., you can feel the Rays' self-loathing. In his book *The Wages of Whiteness*, the historian David Roediger argues that the idea of "whites" and "blacks" as separate "races" helped white people cope with the impoverishment caused by the spread of industrial capitalism. The Rays did not embrace any "ethnic" story that explained this legacy to them as a series of acts of fortitude and resistance in the face of hatred and discrimination. Instead, they saw subtractions, assaults from outsiders to whiteness; above all, from Black people. James Earl Ray was the oldest of nine children. His family eventually settled in Ewing, a small Missouri town where the locals bragged that no Black person had ever spent the night there. They lived in a household with no electricity and burned parts of it to stay warm one especially harsh winter. When he was five years old, his baby sister died in a fire, an event that plunged his mother into mourning, and that led her to neglect her living children.

In the eyes of certain thinkers and observers of United States society from the eighteenth to the twentieth century, people like the Rays were white anomalies. They were of Anglo-Saxon stock—the supposed racial font of the greatness of the United States of America—and yet they endured lives of degradation. These race theorists argued that poor white people of the Midwest and Appalachia possessed biological traits that shaped their behavior and determined their social status. The endemic outcasts of the white United States were racialized by "scientists" who called them "crackers" (in the eighteenth century), and "degenerate" and "the Tribe of Ishmael" (in the nineteenth). One writer traced their origins back to "the old convict stock" expelled from England in the seventeenth century.

The race theories others applied to him were likely unknown to Ray, but he could certainly feel prejudice in the way the others treated him, especially those with whom he was supposed to share a kinship in whiteness. His schoolteacher in the fifth grade in Ewing hated him and seemed to have taken a perverse pleasure in describing how filthy his appearance was: "disgusting," "smelling of urine." Ray embarked on a life of petty crime, and this eventually led him to the Missouri State Penitentiary. After he escaped from that institution (hiding under loaves of bread in a prison truck), he eventually headed for what he imagined would be a land of sunshine and reinvention. Los Angeles. He ended up in the integrated "Grade Three" neighborhood of East Hollywood.

———

MY MOTHER WAS SEVERAL MONTHS PREGNANT AND CARRY-
ing the very conspicuous globe of her belly when a Black
man greeted her in the basement laundry of her apartment
building. Booker Wade was taking Spanish classes at nearby
Los Angeles City College. "It doesn't matter what time,
pound on my door," he told her. "I will help you." He may
have noticed my mother's eyes opening wide in amazement
when he said this. For several days before this fateful encounter, she had been praying to a newly canonized Black
saint, Martin of Porres. San Martin was the "illegitimate"
child of a sixteenth-century Spanish nobleman and a freed
slave of African and Indigenous descent in colonial Peru.
The image of him most commonly produced in plastic figures and printed devotional cards is of a Black man in a
friar's frock, an expression of benevolence on his face, the
visage of a man who has suffered the melancholy of race,
and who has become stronger for it. Now, Booker, a Black
man, approached her and offered help. My mother tells me
this was an act of God. I tell her the true miracle is African
American history.

Wade was from Memphis, Tennessee, and when I think
about that city and state, I remember the strands of African
American struggle that wind through there. I think of
W. E. B. Du Bois, the author of *The Souls of Black Folk*, setting
off to the rural hamlets where he became a schoolteacher to
striving Black students, a generation after abolition. And I
think of Ida B. Wells and the mob that destroyed the offices
of her newspaper in 1892 after she dared to suggest that behind the epidemic of lynching in the South there was an
uncomfortable secret: the entirely consensual relationships
between Black men and white women.

As a teenager growing up in Memphis, Booker Wade

became a member of the NAACP, and he joined its youth wing. In 1961, he and other young NAACP activists entered the segregated central branch of the Memphis Public Library, sitting down to read and to peruse the card catalog in an act of silent defiance. Wade and the other protesters were arrested and carried off by three burly white police officers who drove them in circles around Memphis, taunting them, reminding them of Emmett Till, the fourteen-year-old boy who had been lynched six years earlier. After that terrifying incident, Wade's mother put him on a bus for Los Angeles. Like my parents, and like James Earl Ray, Wade had come to Los Angeles as a kind of runaway.

When he met my mother, Booker Wade had recently been elected to the student government at LACC. In December 1962, he and other student leaders met at a private lunch with Martin Luther King Jr. at the college when the civil rights leader spoke there. Today I can imagine Booker in a dark suit and thin tie, with the budding confidence and quivering nerves of a smart nineteen-year-old as he and his fellow students questioned King about Malcolm X and the two leaders' very different ideas about Black resistance.

Booker Wade drove my mother to Los Angeles County General Hospital on a chilly February morning in a convertible with a top that wouldn't go up; he wore a blue suit to my baptism. Later, he moved out of East Hollywood, to the suburbs, where he started a newspaper focused on African American issues, beginning a lifelong career in media.

My parents moved to a nearby duplex at 5424½ Harold Way. This building was demolished long ago, but I can still see it in pictures. I am riding a tricycle before it, in 1967. I'm sitting at a backyard birthday party, surrounded by neighborhood kids, with a cinder-block wall nearby. James

Earl Ray moved into the building behind that wall, at 1535 North Serrano Avenue, a few months later. The assassin-to-be was invisible to me. I am fairly certain my child's eyes never fell upon him, a black-haired man with a grim, hard face, and a taste for sharp-looking clothes. But today I know he was just over the fence, behind the old, unused brick incinerator next to our duplex, on the other side of the jade plants, a fugitive plotting his entry into history.

AT FIRST GLANCE, MY FAMILY'S PLACE INSIDE THIS STORY alongside a principled Black man and a white assassin might seem like a fantastic coincidence. But in a deeper sense, it's completely natural and unsurprising. The story of "Latino" people in the United States is a drama that begins on the stage of "Black" and "white," and all the history and the conflict born of those terms. In this country, "race" hovers over everything we do. And across the United States, Latino people inhabit places that are never far from Black struggle and the history of white supremacy.

I see families gathering for a Cinco de Mayo celebration in Gettysburg, just a few hundred yards down the Emmitsburg Road from the spot where an army assembled in the name of white supremacy charged across an open field in the climactic battle of the Civil War. And in another corner of southern Pennsylvania, in Chambersburg, I see there is a "Mercado Latino" and a Mexican restaurant at the site where John Brown and Frederick Douglass met, two months before Brown's raid on the federal armory at Harpers Ferry. Chambersburg was then, and now, home to a large Black community. John Brown headed off from Chambersburg to attack Harpers Ferry; he thought he would start a guerrilla war that would emancipate thousands of Black people, who would then become an army to fight slavery. His raid failed, and he was captured and executed, but his actions helped trigger the Civil War. And after the Union won that war the United States approved the Fourteenth Amendment, a key document in the life of the future Latino communities of the United States. The first sentence of that amendment made me, and every other child of an immigrant, citizens of the United States at the moment of our births.

IN 1916, THE AUTHOR THOMAS DIXON PURCHASED AN ORANGE grove at the corner of Hollywood Boulevard and Western Avenue, two blocks from my future home. Dixon's novel *The Clansman* celebrated and justified the humiliation of Black people, and he made a great deal of money when D. W. Griffith adapted it into *The Birth of a Nation*, the first Hollywood blockbuster movie. *The Birth of a Nation* helped spread a myth about white victimization at the hands of newly freed Black slaves in the post–Civil War South; it was filmed, in large measure, in an East Hollywood studio a mile from my future home. Dixon took the money he had made from his hugely popular story of white supremacy and built his own movie studio. (It was demolished by the time my family moved in; there was a record store at the site, and I bought my first albums there.)

Dixon's novel and the movie both featured the hooded racist vigilantes of the Ku Klux Klan portrayed as heroes. In the film, actors in blackface play the parts of lecherous freedmen; both the film and the book appeared during a period when the lynching of Black people was endemic in many corners of the United States. *The Clansman* and *The Birth of a Nation* helped spur the resurgence of the Ku Klux Klan in the first decades of the twentieth century; they are fairy tales about race that had murderous consequences in real life.

But the idea of "race" itself, and of "white," is a fairy tale.

The current meaning of race as a group of people with certain shared biological traits has its roots in what historians call "the long sixteenth century," when the spread of mercantile capitalism brought new peoples in contact, creating new inequalities and new forms of exploitation. Race is an idea born from a European history of migration, conquest, domination. The idea of "white" and "Black" races took hold thanks to the Atlantic slave trade; you could say it was created to justify that trade. By the eighteenth century, with Asia, Africa, Europe, and the Americas linked by global trade routes, and the industrial revolution beginning, scientists attempted to classify the "races" of humanity. In Nell Irvin Painter's wonderful book *The History of White People*, you can learn how the term "Caucasian" was born from the accounts of European travelers who visited the Caucasus and brought back stories of the white women enslaved and sold there; they created a mythology of Caucasian women as the epitome of human beauty. The scientist Johann Friedrich Blumenbach invented a scheme to classify humanity into "races" by collecting skulls of people from around the world, including one sent to him by a Moscow anatomist. The skull belonged to a woman from the Caucasus (she had been captured by the Russian army and may have been a sex slave). When Blumenbach measured her skull's proportions he proclaimed it the embodiment of perfection and of the white race. In this fashion, the term

"Caucasian" became a synonym for white. Of the names of the five races Blumenbach "discovered" (the others are Mongoloid, Malayan, Ethiopian, and American), Caucasian is the only one still in common use in English. Caucasian has survived as an idea for centuries because its exotic undertones and pseudoscientific origins help to mask the deep subjectivity of white identity, the fact that "white" is an idea born from feelings, not from science.

DESPITE THE PRESENCE OF THE WORD "CAUCASIAN" ON MY birth certificate, my parents never called themselves that, because doing so would have involved erasing and forgetting people they knew and loved. My mother's father was the deep brown of wet soil and was born in a Guatemalan town that is the center of Kaqchikel Mayan culture. Her sister, my aunt Imelda, is also a dark, mocha brown. In many Latino families (including among my own children), color is a lottery, a roll of the genetic dice, and in the varied hues of brothers and sisters we see echoes of the cross-ethnic encounters of our ancestors. My mother's mother was somewhat lighter than my grandfather, and in her full cheeks and honey-colored eyes I always imagined she had a German ancestor or two. My father's mother had the distinct profile of a Mayan sculpture, and her family hailed from Quetzaltenango and Huehuetenango, the heartland of the Quiché and Mam and other Mayan ethnicities.

Today, our link to indigeneity is a source of pride and power to many people called "Latino." The students I've met who can trace their Indigenous heritage treasure this knowledge, as with a student of mine who was born and raised among the Mixe people of Oaxaca. The Mixe live in mountain communities, and their name is derived from the Nahuatl word for "cloud." My student grew up listening to her parents speak the Mixe language, but today she remembers only the Mixe word for "belly button." Most people called "Latino" have had their connection to the Native peoples of the Americas deliberately erased. None of my grandparents ever admitted to having Mayan ancestors. In previous centuries racial and ethnic mixing was more of a taboo than it is today, of course, and it's common for people with "Latino" heritage to see their family tree as an object of mystery, its trunk and branches hidden by secrets. My grandparents went to their graves holding secrets of encounters between "ladinos" (people of European descent) and "indios"; or perhaps it was their parents and grandparents who carried those secrets.

What Latino people are left with are the words we use to describe the hues in our skins, the shapes of our eyes, the color and curl and the straightness in our hair, the legacy of our ancestors' bold and unsanctioned couplings across racial and ethnic lines. When I visit the places where "Latino" people live I hear people use the many different vocabularies of skin color. Moreno, blanco, prieto, caramelo, canche, white-passing, Black, brown, fair. Latino is, in many ways, a synonym for "mixed," but the even-deeper mixing of our times can leave us feeling unmoored. As one of my Blaxican students writes, quoting her Blaxican sister: "Too white for the Black kids, too Black for the white kids—I'm neither. Sometimes Mexican girls don't like me because I don't speak Spanish. Black girls don't like me because I don't have the same hair." The mixing in our present or in our past leaves us confused and anxious because "race" and "ethnicity" hover over our lives, in the mindset of everyone, rich and poor, educated and uneducated. We know race shapes how people see us, that it is a category into which our bodies and our histories are supposed to belong.

WHEN JAMES EARL RAY WAS MY NEIGHBOR, THE WORD "RACE" had not yet entered my vocabulary; the California light that touched me was pure. I did not know that people saw me differently. I did not know that the world into which I was born was filled with racial classifications, official and unofficial. Epithets that were mumbled and shouted, the categories filled out on the birth certificates and census forms of the late 1960s, tallied in school district and city planning offices.

Like legions of present-day white supremacists, James Earl Ray found a sense of purpose inside his racial identity. Ray came to Los Angeles to reinvent himself as a white American hero, and he planned to kill the most famous Black man in the United States to become one. Today, the "Patriot" movement appropriates the images of the American Revolution (the coiled snake of "Don't Tread on Me," the U.S. flag with thirteen stars in the canton) as symbols of white assertiveness against the threat posed by Black people. Ray also thought of white in this way: white was his war, and it was the idea behind his private project of liberation and self-realization. While he was our neighbor in East Hollywood, he tried his hand at self-improvement; he took classes on hypnotism and dance and bartending, hoping to become the happy and cultured white person he always longed to be. He visited the North Hollywood presidential campaign office of George Wallace, the governor of Alabama who'd become a folk hero among segregationists for his attempt to stop two African American students from entering the University of Alabama.

In 1968, Ray was forty and my father twenty-seven. Ray's education ended in the tenth grade, at age sixteen; my father's schooling in Guatemala ended at the sixth grade, at age eleven. In Los Angeles, while Ray took his self-improvement classes, my father had resumed his education with adult-school courses to earn his high school diploma. My father purchased a used red 1966 Volkswagen, the first car I can remember him owning. On the day I celebrated my fifth birthday, Ray traveled to a Hollywood Boulevard car repair shop a few blocks from my home to pick up the cream-colored 1965 Ford Mustang he'd had serviced there, and that he would later use to drive cross-country to Memphis to kill King.

In East Hollywood, Ray lived in a Grade Three neighborhood among people with backgrounds as needy and hardscrabble as his own. Among Guatemalans, Filipinos, Armenians, Mexicans, and Black people. Throughout his life, Ray often found himself in places of ethnic and racial mixing. He had been born into one, on the 900 block of West Ninth Street in Alton, Illinois. When I look up the 1930 census records for that block (a count taken thirteen months before Ray was born) I see the names of the people who were likely his neighbors at his birth, the people who heard his first days and weeks of newborn wailing. They are Black people, mostly, born in Mississippi and Texas and other southern places, and one woman from Kansas. They list their occupations as "porter" and "laborer" and "laundress." And a woman whose mother hailed from the "Irish

Free State," and a family of speakers of "Austrian German" from Czechoslovakia. Ray spent his life running away from this truth; he was born alongside Black people and "ethnics" at the bottom of the U.S. social pyramid. They were his kin and community as much as the pure white Americans he longed to imitate.

Poor white people have mixed with Black people and other "people of color" since before the United States was founded. In colonial New York City, Black slaves and poor whites were accused of conspiring to burn down the city together, and later assorted racist pundits feared Irish immigrants would mix with African Americans and produce a "mongrel" race. Black and white and Native American people in southern Virginia mixed and procreated with one another throughout the Jim Crow era, despite anti-miscegenation laws designed to protect the purity of the white race; in 1967, a couple with heritage from all three of those groups won a Supreme Court verdict (*Loving v. Virginia*) that abolished those laws. I've seen this mixing myself in many different corners of the United States. I've heard how the Alabama drawl of white and Black folk can stick to a boy born in Mexico but raised in Birmingham. And on a campus in Cincinnati, Ohio, I've met with women of Appalachian heritage who married Latino immigrants and became members of the college's "Latin American student alliance," a kind of Chicano English on the tips of their Appalachian tongues.

AGAIN AND AGAIN IN HIS TRAVELS AND MISADVENTURES across the United States, James Earl Ray saw how close he was to the social station of African Americans and other people of color. The Missouri State Penitentiary was integrated while he was there. When he killed King, he roomed in a hotel that was in a downtrodden corner of Memphis, on the edge of a Black neighborhood, with pawnshops down the street, a neighborhood like so many others in which he'd put his head down to sleep. With bitterness and violence he turned against the truth of his proximity to people of color, and of the tainted nature of his whiteness; from holding a gun in a grocery-store robbery, to a rifle aimed at a prophet of Black liberation.

Today, a certain kind of proud white person seeks to make Latino people miserable because they see us living among them. The assorted groups of self-appointed vigilantes at the border, armed with rifles and binoculars and dressed in Kevlar armor, are the spiritual heirs of James Earl Ray. Like him, they want to make the fairy tale of "white" real again. Our "Mexican" and "Latino" and "illegal" presence brings out the faded colors and rough edges of the timeworn communities in which they live. The hatred they direct toward us is the loathing they feel for themselves.

A similar kind of self-loathing exists inside the home of the "Latino" or "Hispanic" or "Spanish" person who embraces the myth of white. They believe whiteness courses through their veins and seek to assert it; this is an old story, and one that has unfolded across many cultures. The term "Latino" itself carries a history of European assimilationism: it is derived from "Latin America," a term French and other European intellectuals coined in the nineteenth century, during their political and cultural rivalry with British and United States imperialism. On a more intimate level, there is the powerful colorism that poisons relationships inside many Latino families, as it does with other peoples of color the world over. The fair-skinned are granted privileges and love denied to the darker-skinned, because of age-old Eurocentric ideas about beauty and intelligence.

People of Afro-Latino heritage suffer the micro- and macro-aggressions of their own family members; of those who see themselves, expressly or without words, as "white." My Blaxican student writes of the moment her parents met, and when her Mexican mother-to-be brought her Black father-to-be to meet her Mexican family—no one spoke to them. In "Reflections about Race by a Negrito Acomplejao," the Afro–Puerto Rican sociologist Eduardo Bonilla-Silva writes: "Very early on in my life I noticed that I received less affection from my immediate and extended family than did my siblings . . . I pondered things no child should ponder: Why doesn't *mami* love me as much as Pedro or Karen? Why do my White family members (at the time, I did not see them as White but just as family) seem so distant?" He describes the "soft" segregation of the dark- and the light-skinned at family gatherings, the language his aunts used to demean Black people. Like my student's family, the Bonilla-Silva family was in denial about the racial mixing in their present and in their past. To be a Latino or Latinx person is to be a "mulatto," a mestizo, and to have a personal history defined, like James Earl Ray's, by its proximity to Blackness and the deep brown of the Indigenous.

The push and pull toward and away from whiteness is one of the defining elements of Latino history. The people now known as Latino seem to be perpetually on the brink of being the next group assimilated into whiteness (following the Jews, Italians, and other groups), only to be racialized as a dark other. In the United States of the first half of the twentieth century, you could travel through Texas and see signs that said NO MEXICANS OR DOGS ALLOWED, alongside the Jim Crow signage that harassed and threatened Black people. When Mexican American activists created their first national organization, they called themselves the League of United Latin American Citizens, in part because they rejected the common insult "Mexican" had become. The U.S. military classified Mexican American soldiers as white in World War II, and thus granted them a privilege denied to African Americans: the right to serve, and die, alongside white soldiers; at the same time, Puerto Rican soldiers of darker complexion were deemed Black and placed in segregated units with African Americans. In the most famous school desegregation case involving Latino students, *Mendez v. Westminster*, Mexican American activists in Orange County, California, sued in federal court in 1946 to end segregation in a public school system; they argued that Mexican students should be allowed to attend white schools because Mexican people were white. In the years before the U.S. authorities militarized and technologized the border with Mexico, white-passing immigrants often crossed the frontier without presenting documents.

Today, there are "Latino" people who try to buy whiteness and protect it with skin-lighteners and plastic surgery and parasols. And there are Latino leaders who work to build political fiefdoms while privately denigrating Black and Indigenous people. They judge or feel themselves superior because of their perceived proximity to "white." They think of their whiteness as a source of power, or as a shield.

Our relationship as Latinos to whiteness is the tragedy and the comedy of us.

THE SHOT JAMES EARL RAY FIRED AT MARTIN LUTHER KING JR. in Memphis did not bring about the white renaissance he envisioned. In Ray's final years, before he died in prison in 1998, he asked to be cremated and to have his ashes scattered in Ireland. He was just one-eighth Irish, and one can read all sorts of motives into this request. Perhaps it was a sorrowful assertion of his humanity, one that attached his family's story to an "ethnic" people whose suffering and achievements in the United States no one could question. Or maybe he was simply seeking to make one final, pathetic assertion of his whiteness by claiming a homeland he perceived to be a paragon of white identity.

THE ASSASSINATION OF MARTIN LUTHER KING JR. TRANSformed the meaning of my middle name, Martin. I had been named for a Peruvian mixed-race saint, but now Martin became a link, in my family's mythos, to African American history—I was named for a great martyr of Black resistance. Black history offered the example of struggle, of unity, of speaking truth against racial hatreds. After I delivered a fiery graduation speech at my college commencement, my father declared, in a moment of parental hyperbole: "I knew one day you'd give a speech like Martin Luther King!"

"ANY FOOL CAN SEE THAT THE WHITE PEOPLE ARE NOT REALLY white, and that black people are not black," the African

American critic Albert Murray wrote in 1970. "They are all interrelated one way or another." Murray argued that the aesthetic of jazz, a musical form born in African American communities, was a dominant force in the shaping of United States culture. (Today, hip-hop plays the same function.) He believed that United States culture was, in its essence, the product of racial mixing, "even in its most rigidly segregated precincts . . . It is, regardless of all the hysterical protestations of those who would have it otherwise, incontestably mulatto. Indeed, for all their traditional antagonisms and obvious differences, the so-called black and so-called white people of the United States resemble nobody else in the world so much as they resemble each other."

A half century after Murray wrote those words, we can say that the United States is as much a mestizo country as it is a mulatto country. The modern United States is a country conflicted over its own mestizo identity, by its mixing with Latin American immigrants and their descendants. This is the newest chapter in the long, sordid, and strange history of the United States and the idea of "race." The migrant mother who crossed a desert, who launched her life in a Latino barrio, moves to a neighborhood where she becomes the white supremacist's neighbor; she takes a job where she becomes his coworker; she becomes the mother of his daughter-in-law. The white patriarch meets his new "Mexican" relatives, his new consuegros, at the gender-reveal party of his future grandchild. The mestizo is a known entity, and she is a mystery. The mestizo is in our speech, in the spiced food the locals devour in the Mexican restaurants to be found in even the smallest rural and remote towns of Oregon, Wyoming, or Maine. Latinidad is in the warm abrazo we give our best buddies. And the Latino is an "alien," a member of that caste of laborers, farmworkers, and servants to be found in all fifty of the United States. And very often she works alongside us in our homes, holding our children, gazing into the cabinets in our bathrooms, a witness to the joys and the frustrations of our daily lives. This fifty-state, sea-to-shining-sea intimacy with Latino people, and "white" America's acceptance and rejection of it, is the force holding the United States together, and tearing it apart.

6

INTIMACIES

In her book *The Maid's Daughter*, the sociologist Mary Romero describes the close relationship between a Beverly Hills family and their live-in Mexican housekeeper and nanny. The father of the "Smith" family is a Hollywood agent, and he and his wife have four children who are fed and cared for by "Carmen." (All the names in the books are pseudonyms.) Carmen's daughter "Olivia" lives with her in the maid's quarters, and in this way the family is a microcosm of the social landscape of the United States; six "white" people and two Mexicans, together under one roof, the darker subservient to the lighter, but also dependent on one another, and intimately familiar with one another. Olivia sleeps in the maid's quarters, sharing a bed with her mother. But Carmen does much of the work raising the four Smith children, and the servant has an authority over them their parents do not; in some ways, Olivia will observe four decades later, the Smith children shed parts of their white privilege and became "Mexican." And the Smiths, in turn, help to raise Olivia; among other things, they pay for Olivia to attend the same private schools as the Smith children.

In the Smith household, employees and bosses become one big family. And, as in all families, the attachments and the resentments among them become more intricate and messier as the five children grow up. The sons and daughters of the Smiths grow distant from their father and his ambition. When Olivia reaches adolescence, she pushes back against the Smiths for their attempts to integrate her into their social lives; she's a brown girl, and she can never fit in at their Beverly Hills debutante cotillions. Carmen believes she is losing her daughter to Mr. and Mrs. Smith and grows distant from her, but she becomes closer to the Smith children; when she discovers a small marijuana stash while cleaning the bedroom of one of the boys, she hides it . . . And so forth, and so on. The story becomes a biracial and bi-ethnic melodrama that ends with some supreme ironies. As a teenager, Olivia embraces her mestiza and Chicana identities, but after she goes off to college she becomes a public relations executive and comes closer to following in Mr. Smith's professional footsteps than any of his children do; as he is dying, Mr. Smith expresses his fatherly love for her. Two of the Smith children, having squandered much of the privilege bequeathed to them, start an office-cleaning business, making a living emptying out the trash bins of others.

The drama of white-Latino contact is not yet a part of the United States' image of itself. In the 1960s, as the United States came to terms with the "mulatto" heritage Albert Murray saw, legions of Black and white people marched side by side for civil rights, and American cinema produced classics such as *In the Heat of the Night* and *Guess Who's Coming to Dinner*, in which Black and white people work out their feelings for one another. This process is still playing itself out today, and reaching ever-deeper levels of intimacy, as in the theater work *Slave Play*, in which present-day Black and white couples argue over the legacy of racism and their ability to achieve orgasm. But the full, tangled drama of the intimate relationships between Latino and white people remains a kind of national secret, an unspoken truth.

The encounters in the homes where Latina domestics work, and in the stores and warehouses and office buildings where Latino and white people labor side by side, are not giving birth to works celebrated in the media as cathartic, culture-shifting American art. Why? Because the white United States is not yet ready to accept the presence of Latino people in the most intimate corners of American life. Instead, in the communities where they watch each other's comings and goings across driveways and front porches and stoops, those encounters are weaponized. A white woman hires a housekeeper who comes to her home once a week and notices the Honduran woman spending a moment or two studying her family pictures, and the first time she sees her doing this it's unsettling because she can feel this stranger learning something about her that is private and that belongs to her. She remembers the voices on cable television, in social media, and on talk radio telling her to fear these people from the south, who've come to her in "caravans" and over fences. A midwesterner remembers these same voices, and the speeches of a nativist President too, as he enters in the Kwik Trip or the Super Stop and sees another customer in a mechanic's uniform with a stitched name patch that says "Pedro"; and for a moment he wonders how and why it is that this brown man has entered the space of his daily routine.

If you've internalized a "white" way of thinking, the

presence of the mestizo outsider on your property, or in your neighborhood, violates your sense of privacy. The eyes of the "Mexican" or "Latin" person in your orbit feel like a camera broadcasting from your kitchen and your bedroom. You feel exposed. The propagandists of white identity tap into this unease and build power and profit from it. They say that white people risk losing something about themselves by their contact with these outsiders. "White" is an idea that does, in fact, begin to lose its power and become meaningless when dark and alien (and supposedly inferior) people enter its domestic and quotidian spaces. In the Smith household ethnic and racial hierarchies began to melt, bleed, and blend into one another—as they do, today, in many other corners of the United States, where the mixing of peoples can make racial and ethnic categories feel increasingly archaic and absurd. Our closeness to one another, the feelings and the insights that develop inevitably when we learn about each other and come to admire and love and respect one another, can show us how much untruth there is in racist thinking.

THE SELF-IMAGE OF THE "WHITE" AMERICAN MIDDLE CLASS, as depicted in film and on television ad nauseam, begins with a block of large, orderly homes with big lawns. The kind you might see decorated with plastic reindeer at Christmastime, holiday lights dangling from the pitched roofs. Or the curving suburban tract of an early Spielberg drama, with cul-de-sacs and boys pumping the pedals on their bicycles to go faster. When the movie camera enters into the homes themselves, we see carpeted spaces, and polished dining-room tables, and mom at work in the kitchen in heels and an apron.

When I wander into these neighborhoods in real life, they do, in fact, have the otherworldly feel of a movie set: the sculpted bushes and trees you see in the most affluent corners of Southern California and southern Connecticut. The newly painted wood of a ranch-style home in tonier neighborhoods of suburban Arizona; the windows freshly washed, reflecting back mirror images of trimmed oaks and maples in greater Denver. I am taken in by the constructed perfection, disposable incomes spent creating scenic paintings in three dimensions. The magic here is that it all seems effortless. No one is sweating in these neighborhoods, unless they're in jogging clothes, working out to make their bodies as taut and chiseled as the landscape around them. Finally, I turn a corner, and I see a pickup truck with scratched skin and garden rakes and shovels arranged in the back, and then another pickup, spick-and-span, with a logo sticker on the door that announces the presence of a team of construction workers employed by a family-run business with a Spanish surname. Or a landscaping business named for a state or city in Mexico. I see a woman of Indigenous features, with weary eyes, walking down the street in her everyday work clothes, headed to the bus stop, and I can feel the clean kitchen counters and the scrubbed faces of the white girls and boys she's left in her wake. At the end of the day, the pickups and the maids file out, taking their Mexican and Central American and Caribbean and South American bodies out of these places, and the fleets of bloated SUVs file in, bringing in the lords of these magnificent properties.

In the class structure of this country, the role of Latino people is to build the movie set of white perfection again and again. We see our mothers and fathers head out each morning to perform this work, when night is still darkening the dawn sky. The effort of erasing Latino labor from the self-image of the middle and upper classes subtracts from the United States' knowledge of itself, placing affluent American families in a kind of dreamspace untethered from grim and unpleasant socioeconomic realities. The Spanish-speaking help appears only fleetingly in their family photographs, if at all. The public image of the privileged is an illusion of affluence and control, and mastery of their surroundings. They would have us believe they summon the gleam and order of their gated communities and suburban "estates" with a mere snap of their fingers, a wink of their eye, like the famous, benevolent blonde witch of a bygone television sitcom.

Every day, Latino people help create the illusion of the effortlessness of pampered whiteness. We are very much conscious of ourselves in this role. It shapes our self-image. A witty Latinx undergrad creates a meme from a photograph of a group of Latino gardeners attacking a leaf-covered street with leaf blowers: the caption declares, LET ME SING YOU THE SONG OF MY PEOPLE. We Latino laborers drive and walk away from the perfect suburban neighborhood at the end of the workday with a sense of satisfaction. Many of us have seen these spacious structures rise from empty lots thanks to our own labor with hammers and saws. But white people quickly forget our brown presence (unless we've broken a dish, or mangled the tricky business of trimming the lawn). They internalize the sense of achievement that comes from the labor we've performed to create spaces that are uncluttered, polished, vacuumed. But we live with the knowledge of a powerful truth: work and muscle are the basis of everything. We know where the beams are inside the walls; we have wiped the soiled face of a stranger's bright child in our care, and heard her speak her first word. We've stood on the roof and seen and repaired the cracked asphalt tiles that keep the family inside dry and warm. Whereas the people who employ us enter their perfect, mortgaged spaces and practice an act of self-delusion every day; because in erasing us from their minds they deny how interdependent we are. As individuals, we are disposable to them; but we know that, as a collectivity, as a class of people, we are irreplaceable. Without us, without the labor of people of color, without our farmworkers and our mechanics, the citizens of the United States would wallow in their own filth and their cars would not run and their toilets would not flush.

We, as "darker" people, as outsiders and newcomers, are forced to study white people, as people of color have since the idea of whiteness and color were invented.

MY STUDENTS TELL STORIES OF THEIR FAMILY LANDSCAPING businesses, of accompanying their fathers as they sweep through suburban neighborhoods with lawnmowers; and of working alongside their mothers on cleaning jobs, or with their aunts and uncles on forays into office buildings to empty trash bins and clean toilets. My students have listened to their elders lecture them—in Spanish, Nahuatl, Mixtec, and English—on the value of hard work and punctuality, and they write stories for me that unfold in those perfect suburban neighborhoods, and also in the imperfect Grade Three or Grade Four corners of the city where Latino people live. They are on a journey across the barriers of class and ethnicity, and they've heard and read what the right-wing pundits call us: "filthy." What a rich and deep irony there is in the single word of that insult and lie. Because we have spent lifetimes literally cleaning the shit of others, sterilizing, bleaching, leaving the ammonia scent of chemical solvents in our wake.

"LATINOS" ARE ONLY THE LATEST GROUP TO LIVE AND WORK in intimate contact with "whites," and to be assigned a legal and social status that separates them from the protections of whiteness. Before the arrival of African people, the principal terms of ethnic division in English North America were between "Christians" and "non-Christians" (i.e., Europeans and Native peoples). "White" became a legal category in seventeenth-century North America after the arrival of enslaved people from Africa. Like the Smiths and Olivia and Carmen, the relationships between "white" masters and "Negro" servants in the English Americas were complicated and messy. In the first few decades after African people arrived on the North American continent there were few legal distinctions between white and Black servants. "There is no doubt that the earliest Negroes in Virginia occupied a position similar to that of the white servants in the colony," the pioneering historian John Hope Franklin wrote. Then the first laws were passed to enforce slavery's new "race" thinking. In 1662, the colonial legislature in Virginia decreed that a child born to a white father and an enslaved Black woman did not inherit the free status of his father; he was a slave, like his mother. Teaching slaves to read and write became illegal, and it was decreed that slaves would require written permission to travel on roads and highways. The drafting of these laws implies behaviors by white and Black people that undermined the order of the new slaveholding society. Clearly, some masters were teaching slaves to read, and others allowed their slaves to travel freely from one town to the next. Some masters set their slaves free, and many of these liberated people purchased property. And free Englishmen conceived children with their slaves; before the new race law were enacted, the traditions of English common law meant those children inherited the free status of their father. As the colonial economy became more dependent on African labor, the idea that people were "white" and "Black" spread, and even more laws were passed defining the differences between the legal rights of Black and white people.

The ideologues of whiteness have long told white people that their true, natural state is to live in an Eden of order and purity, emotionally and culturally separate from the Negroes, Puerto Ricans, aliens, and the other dark people who feed them, who clean up after them, and who build things for them. In the slave system, the contradictions inherent in this way of thinking began to tear at the nation's conscience and its ethical fabric. The country's moral conflict over slavery sparked more laws and rulings trying to enforce race discipline, culminating with the infamous Dred Scott decision, in which the chief justice of the Supreme Court boiled down the race thinking of white supremacy to its essence: Black people were not citizens and "had no rights which the white man was bound to respect."

Throughout United States history the ways this country organizes labor and produces wealth have shaped our ideas and our laws about "race" and "aliens." In the twentieth and twenty-first centuries, as the number of Latino laborers in U.S. homes and on farms and in other workplaces increased, the laws defining "alien" status grew more numerous and complex. The historian Natalia Molina describes this process at length in her work on "racial scripts" about immigrant people. In my lifetime I've seen the creation of several new categories of immigration status (TPS, DACA, etc.), and the invention of a new term to describe the uncomfortable legal situation in millions of American homes: "mixed-status families." I've seen immigration laws become harsher and more inhuman, until finally the United States created camps and cells for detained children. In effect, this country's immigration laws seek to teach the American people to keep race discipline and to punish Latino immigrants because so many families and employers have come to depend on them and trust them, and because the United States cannot eat without Latino labor. (According to a U.S. Department of Agriculture study, roughly half of the men and women hired to pick crops in this country are undocumented immigrants.)

The history of white privilege is of race demagogues and the state building ever more elaborate laws and race theories to enforce and encourage the disciplined obedience to racist treatment of "the Other"—while simultaneously the intimate contacts between the races in homes and workplaces eat away at the idea of racial difference. Put another way, a society whose economy is based on inequalities of "race" has to teach its citizens to keep race discipline because otherwise a troublesome minority will treat their "inferiors" like human beings. This dynamic once played out in homes where slave owners and their human "property" lived, including in the homes of many of the nation's "founding fathers."

Today, legions of upper- and middle-class residents of the United States hire undocumented Latin American immigrant women to work in their homes, and don't ask for papers. They benefit from the low wages an immigrant is forced to accept, and derive a sense of privilege from being able to contract some or all of their parental and domestic duties to those immigrants. At the same time, the passage of the months and years in which they remain in close contact with these employees makes their shared humanity all the more obvious. White women form powerful emotional bonds with their Latin American nannies and take pride in the Spanish words they and their children have learned. Such white families often do things that explicitly attack or undermine the nation's immigration laws; they might place NO HUMAN BEING IS ILLEGAL stickers on their cars, or provide the cash their employees need to smuggle a relative into the United States. And they might do these things even as they send their children to private schools, where they are insulated from the perceived dysfunctions of the poor, "people of color" masses.

As complicated as these relationships are, the intimacies among the peoples called "Latino" and "white" and "Black" tend to undermine, in the long run, the ideological and emotional foundations of whiteness as an idea.

ONE CONSTANT IN AMERICAN HISTORY HAS BEEN THE INVENtion of new ethnicities, new racial prejudices to justify the inequalities of capitalist growth. Each new prejudice is built on the basis of old ones. Before the Irish became the butt of nineteenth-century American racism, they were debased by British colonialism. Likewise with the Poles, the Slovaks, the Germans, and others kicked around the potato and wheat fields of Europe by assorted lords and ethnic foes for generations. Today, immigrants from Latin America and generations of their progeny form a de facto caste of service labor. As with their Polish, German, and Irish predecessors, these laborers are living with legacies of the race and caste thinking that predate their families' arrival in the United States.

In the middle of the city of Los Angeles, I meet a woman whose native language is Nahuatl; she learned Spanish in the United States, and then a smattering of English, her third tongue. Julia Rodriguez has three children and she lives in a one-room apartment in a tenement, the kind of building that rose in the first decades of the twentieth century to house immigrants from the Ottoman, Russian, and Austro-Hungarian empires, and transplants from needy corners of the United States. Now, in the early twenty-first century, this building is a Black and brown place. She and her children sleep in two sets of bunk beds in that one room, a sink and stove opposite them, along with a small table at which the family shares meals and where her children do their homework. Julia grew up in Guerrero, Mexico. As a woman and an Indigenous person from a rural village, she lived a multilayered oppression, a Mexican intersectionality. Patriarchy has long derived its power from depriving women of education; in rural Mexico, a father might declare, "What's the use in educating a daughter if it's only to write love letters to her boyfriend," and the result is a young woman more pliable to a patriarch's orders. Often, daughters are put to work to save money for the education of their brothers.

Like many rural women in Latin America, Julia never went to school. She never learned to read and write. Now she tells me what it was like to be thirty-two years old and analfabeta, and then to finally sit in a classroom and have all the words around her, on street signs and school permission slips, be suddenly decoded and filled with meaning. "I was asleep before," Julia tells me in Spanish. "Before, there was no sun for me. Now I feel más despierta." When she reads, she is fully awake. Julia is one of three adults I interview who arrived in Los Angeles illiterate and who were quickly incorporated into the world of service and other low-paid labor, working for decades in the United States without ever learning to read and write. One is a Hollywood house-keeper in her sixties, another a restaurant cook, also in his sixties. In the United States they worked and stayed in low-paying jobs with zero prospect of advancement. Illiteracy encircled and silenced them, surrounding them with walls of undecipherable symbols that mocked them; it was the most potent symbol of their oppression, of the way their class status infantilized them in the tech-centric culture of the United States. They had been victimized by forms of oppression that were very new, and also very old. As a boy, Juan Contreras, the cook, was lent out by his father to work on plantations and pay off his father's debts; he was a ten-year-old whose family was trapped in the ancient form of exploitation known as debt peonage. Then he was impris-oned in that modern American form of exploitation called the service economy. White privilege in the United States is a conspiracy between old forms exploitation and new ones, the plantation and country lords of one century lending a hand to the garment-factory owner and food-processing corporation of another.

With the barriers of class ever more rigid in this coun-try, the labor of Julia and others can make them feel like Sisyphus, the son of a Greek king. Each day, at work, she rolls a boulder up a hill; illiteracy and undocumented status, all the class and gendered oppression she's suffered, make the boulder roll back downhill, and she finds herself back where she started, in a tenement room in the center of Los Angeles, raising three children, alone, because their father was deported. Mexican patriarchy and United States capitalism conspired to keep her illiterate. Permanent poverty is the fate that seems to haunt us, to hover over us. It can be the fate of the undocumented, for whom the laws targeting their "alien" status form real, legal barriers to advancement. Our Sisyphean labors can go on for generations, as we are stratified and barrio-ized into a laboring caste.

WE ROLL A BOULDER TO THE TOP OF A HILL, AND IT ROLLS down. The futility of the moment fits with the message of suffering and humility delivered to us by bitter and excessively pious Catholic relatives, and by high school teachers who seem to enjoy telling us we'll never amount to anything. But sometimes the boulder stays there in place at the top of the hill after we've rolled it up there with our Indigenous and mestizo and Latinx stubbornness and muscle. As if by magic. And suddenly we are standing at the top of a tower of stones we've built, and we look around and see the panorama of our labors. We see the Sisyphus metaphor for what it really is: an old folktale, whispered from one Greek to the next, written on parchment, retold in children's books, a story that cannot and does not define us.

When I sit and listen to Julia Rodriguez, in the one-room apartment alongside her three children, I feel I have entered a space of order and achievement and safety. In less than two hundred square feet. I feel the effort it's taken to build this home in the universe of precarity that surrounds it. Beyond the room's only door, there is the hallway outside, with a thin carpet made thinner by generations of tenant footsteps, and windows at either end of the hallway leading to old iron fire escapes, and to the territory of the local drug dealers. The hallway and the walls of her apartment fill with the noise of dozens of people living alongside and on top of one another. Julia asks me if I'd like something to drink, and of course I say yes, and I sit down at the small table and accept the canned soda she offers, and I take my notebook and ask her questions. I'm meeting her just a few months after she's learned to read and write, and she is still living inside the aura of the miracle and marvel of this newfound skill. Even walking around the city is different. "I know what street I'm standing on. And I can look for the name of the street I'm going to." She reads the letters from her children's school and, most recently, a book on child development she found at the local branch of the public library. She tells me she wished she had read it as a teenager. "That book would have helped me a lot. But now when my children get bigger, I know what to expect."

The day after I write a newspaper column about Julia Rodriguez and the other newly literate immigrants I've met, my father arrives at my home and announces, "I have something to tell you." He reveals a truth he's been hiding since he was a boy. His mother, my grandmother, the late Valeria Cruz, never learned to read or write. He shows me a copy of her Guatemala passport, the document she used when she came to visit us in the United States: there is an X on the signature line, and a notation by a Guatemalan bureaucrat: "Ignora firmar." Doesn't know how to sign. Her illiteracy was the great shame of his life. When he was a teenager he tried to teach her some letters, but she resisted: *It's too late for me now*, she said. When I was a boy, my father photographed me alongside books, an image of learning and achievement, and he filled up our house with books, including the novels of the Guatemalan writer Miguel Ángel Asturias, who had just won the Nobel Prize. In his twenties and thirties my father was a service-worker intellectual, parking cars and standing behind a hotel reception desk, and reading books in his free time. When I was a boy, he took me to Pickwick Books on Hollywood Boulevard (where the future essayist and critic Susan Sontag had been caught shoplifting *Doctor Faustus* as a teenager). At this bookstore he bought me the first expensive gift I can remember receiving from him: a big, heavy, hardcover copy of *The American Heritage Dictionary of the English Language*, first edition. A man whose mother could not read a word in any language had given his son all the words in English. I recognized in that dictionary, with its copious illustrations and pithy and illuminating etymologies, a work of beauty and power.

In Julia's house, I see her ten-year-old son reading Harry Potter; her nine-year-old is reading girl-detective stories; and her six-year-old is devouring early reader books. "Tim spins," the girl reads. "Tim spins his hat." The outsider sees the Julia Rodriguezes of an American city step on a bus and leave the affluent, perfect corners of that metropolis. Their vision of her life ends with her at that suburban bus stop. They imagine her entering the grimy and overpopulated warrens of the immigrant barrio. No one pretends there is perfection in these crowded and transient places. But what is the true story here? Tragedy, melodrama, epic, pathos?

In Julia's apartment I see a woman and her three children, sleeping and living in intimate and close contact, like stowage passengers on a ship. They make the bunk beds every morning, and Julia cooks breakfast and dinner on that small stove, and she combs her sons' hair and washes her daughter's stretchy pants. I imagine them entering this space after their trek to the library. Julia tells me she's just purchased her first book: a guide to praying the rosary. How will Julia's children grow into the world, how will they see and understand this story they lived? Will they carry pride or bitterness at being witnesses to their mother's labors? I wonder how much and how clearly they will remember the moment when she seized the opportunity to read and write. And if they will remember the day when she wanted to give up and stop going to her classes, and her oldest told her, "No, mommy, you have to go back."

I am reminded of another interview I did in a one-room apartment with a woman who raised her children alone: Esperanza Monterrosa, a housekeeper from El Salvador. From the Echo Park district of Los Angeles, she took the number 2 bus every weekday westward, stepping off on Doheny Drive in Beverly Hills, the very summit of American affluence. Sometimes her daughter Cinthia would join her on these work trips, and help out at the mansion where Esperanza worked. Then one day Cinthia took the same bus, but did not get off on Doheny: instead, she took it several more stops westward to the campus of UCLA, where she eventually became the first Latina elected student-body president. A friend of Esperanza tells me: "I always said, 'That girl is going to be on TV one day . . . She's going to break the chains for all of us.'" A decade after her graduation, and a few years after receiving her law degree, Cinthia is appointed by the governor of California to a state commission that protects the rights of farmworkers. She calls me for advice on publicizing a judgment the commission has made, a case that has reached the United States Supreme Court.

The impulse to question and challenge class and ethnic barriers is a powerful and enduring one. When we move to "break the chains" by doing something as simple or as grand as learning to read and write, or filing a writ with the U.S. Supreme Court, we enter an exalted state. We are free of the self-delusions of the affluent, and we have liberated ourselves of the hopelessness of caste. We see our country as it truly is. Juan Contreras, who was a debt peon at ten, tells me what he discovered when he learned to read, in his sixties. The stories in the city's Spanish-language newspaper, *La Opinión*, were especially illuminating. "It's really sad how many atrocities there are going on in the world," he tells me. "But there are some nice things too, like when you read about people trying to help others." Once, he had navigated his way around Los Angeles by studying and memorizing the small imperfections in street signs he could not read. As a reader, the street signs came into focus, and the world and its interconnected relationships took on new meanings. This is the story of an entire people. The epic of our awakening, from peons to readers to citizens, our coming into knowledge and power. Our journey into a truth fuller than our oppressors can ever know. It's why you're reading this book, and all the words you read before.

WHEN I WAS A BOY, I TOOK MY FIRST JOURNEYS ACROSS THE class divide of my city and country. My aunt Gladys worked as a housekeeper for a Beverly Hills family; in the summer, this family often took vacations in Europe and my aunt would invite us over, and my father, his wife, myself, and my two cousins would have the run of this property for an afternoon. We would swim in their pool, which was surrounded by bird-of-paradise plants, palm trees, and a green lawn. Sometimes I would wander into the home itself, alone, into what was, to my child's eye, a palace of rooms; long corridors with one door leading to one room, and then another, and another. I would see many portraits of the members of this white family, with their pink cheeks and tall, lean frames; and one room dedicated entirely to a drum set. I remember entering the kitchen, and living rooms, spaces with marble counters and the woven rugs and delicate vases, each as still and as appealing to the eye as a museum exhibit.

I remember the last time I visited that Beverly Hills house. I had left Los Angeles to go away to college and then returned to become a newspaper reporter, at the age of twenty-five. My aunt was the home's summer caretaker, again, and she invited me over. For the first time I saw that "mansion" with adult eyes. It was a rather unassuming home, small by Beverly Hills standards. When I parked my car I saw that the driveway was not the wide, curved space I remembered. Once inside the house, I walked through just two or three rooms and exited the home into the backyard. Time had caused that palace to shrink into something the size of a bungalow. Its hugeness was an illusion created in my mind's eye by the smallness I felt then, the smallness of a brown boy who felt he was an interloper, a secret trespasser inside someone else's dream.

My two cousins grew up and went to college; the older one graduated from the UCLA dentistry school and the younger one from USC's medical school. Their mother died some years ago. Now they don't speak to each other: it's a long, complex, and not always happy family story. But I often think of my aunt and her ambition: among other things, she and her husband bought a small home just across a wide boulevard from the Beverly Hills border in the 1970s, and they eventually started their own housekeeping business. The doctor who owned the Beverly Hills home where she worked died a few years ago. My older cousin says he was a great and generous man, and that he helped both her and my aunt receive their permanent U.S. residency—and that he once performed a surgery on my aunt's ailing mother, for free. The doctor's obituary listed a life of achievements on two continents, the names of his children and step-children, all the businesses he had founded, the medical procedures he had pioneered, his hobbies, the skiing championships he had won as a young man, the half dozen hospitals at which he had worked, and where he took his vacations. But it did not, of course, mention my Guatemalan aunt and her decades of labor at his home, and the kindnesses he performed for her family. She was absent from his public history.

WE LATINO, LATINX, AND HISPANIC PEOPLE HAVE OUR OWN absences and erasures. My aunt had secrets, painful details about her Guatemalan childhood she would never have wanted recorded in her own obituary. Among other things, she was ashamed of her teeth, many of which she had lost during her youth in Guatemala, and which her daughter the dentist later repaired and replaced.

One day soon, a flood of our Latino, Latinx, Hispanic,

Afro-Latino, and Indigenous secrets will enter the public realm and begin to shape the United States' perception of itself. When that day comes, a migrant mother with a desert crossing in her past will enter an American movie theater, or a bookstore, or wander into a Broadway theater, and see her pain, and the complexity of her relationship to the "white" people of the United States and all its secrets represented in a renaissance of creative work. A "Barrio Renaissance" like the Harlem Renaissance of the last century.

For now, however, that migrant mother can wander into the Museum of Modern Art in New York, the National Museum of Women in the Arts in Washington, D.C., or the San Francisco Museum of Modern Art and see paintings by an artist whose work has come to represent for many Americans the psychological and cultural turbulence of "Latinidad." She was an artist not widely celebrated during her lifetime, who worked against the erasures of her pain, the absence of her presence, her heritage, and of women's stories from the public culture to which she was born. An artist whose work was defined by the uncovering of family secrets, and whose paintings are today valued in the millions of dollars.

7

SECRETS

In the 1980s and '90s, as the term "Latino" spread thanks to new waves of migration from Latin America, symbols of Latino culture became widely popular among young people. They bought objects that expressed their Latinidad, and they decorated their bedrooms, dorm rooms, and living rooms with them. The most ubiquitous of these symbols were self-portraits painted by a Mexican artist of European complexion and ethnically ambiguous features. In countless posters and postcards and stickers, this woman of German-Jewish and Oaxacan-Indigenous descent wears huipiles and Tehuantepec headdresses and other folk creations of Mexico's Native peoples.

Frida Kahlo remains today one of the most commonly invoked symbols of Latinidad in the United States. She has been canonized and her work commodified. Kahlo's popularity first spread in the United States some thirty years after her death, when she was rehabilitated as a feminist icon, a symbol of the power and presence of women in a field—painting—forever dominated by European men. Latino people adopted her at a time when more of us were rejecting the idea that we should assimilate into Anglo-Saxon Protestant culture. The Kahlo boom swept across the United States along with Day of the Dead celebrations and the founding of university departments of Chicano, Puerto Rican, and Latino studies.

Latinx people connect with Kahlo's art and her persona because her art invites us to enter the intimate spaces of her subconscious, the physical and emotional torments she endured, and her ethnic identity.

Frida Kahlo's ethnicity is a story as complex as that of your typical Latinx resident of New York, Miami, or Los Angeles. In the painting *My Grandparents, My Parents, and I*, a naked child Frida stands before the house in Coyoacán, Mexico, where she was born, a red ribbon connecting her to portraits of her parents and grandparents. Her very prieto grandfather is on the upper left; he was a man of "Indian" extraction (her biographers are never more specific than that) and was born in Morelia, but later migrated to Oaxaca, where he married the daughter of a general of "Spanish" extraction. Frida's very fair-skinned, muttonchopped Hungarian grandfather is on the upper right of the painting; he and his wife migrated from Transylvania to Germany, and their son (Frida's father) migrated to Mexico, where he met Frida's mother and changed his name from Wilhelm to Guillermo. *My Grandparents, My Parents, and I* depicts a migration story of cross-racial and cross-ethnic intimacies. Kahlo placed her mestiza mother in the center of the canvas, wearing a wedding dress, while inside her a fetus Frida is waiting to be born. One scholar has compared this, and other Kahlo works, to the eighteenth-century casta portraits of mixed-race Mexican families.

In interviews and in the many letters she wrote during

the course of her lifetime, Frida Kahlo did not claim Indigenous identity. But she recognized indigeneity as part of her being, and as an integral element of Mexican identity. In *The Two Fridas* she depicts herself as two women; one in a Tehuana dress and the other in a Victorian dress. In most of her self-portraits she wore huipiles, rebozos, and jade jewelry, all created by or inspired by Indigenous people. In one of her most striking self-portraits, she is wearing a flower-shaped Tehuana headdress. Many a present-day critic has called this "cultural appropriation." But members of Frida's mother's family were wearing such Indigenous clothing long before Frida was born. In an 1890 photograph taken in Oaxaca, her mestiza mother, Matilde Calderón y González (then age seven), sits for a group portrait. The young Matilde wears an Indigenous dress and is surrounded by relatives who are prieto and blanco and the many shadings in between. The women are wearing embroidered faldas and Tehuana headdresses. It's a portrait of a racially mixed family embracing symbols of their indigeneity—at a time when the Mexican government was engaged in wars against Indigenous peoples on both its southern and northern borders.

For Kahlo, the photographs of her Oaxacan family were one more piece of the puzzle of her story. She also told people she had Jewish ancestors (though later biographers found this to be untrue), and she collected books on the tortures suffered by the Jews during the Spanish Inquisition; she may have been referencing those torments in a 1945 painting depicting herself on a bed, being force-fed after a failed operation on her spine. In the same way that children of Latin American migrants study Spanish and scan the internet to learn about the culture of their ancestors and the violence those ancestors endured in Latin America, Kahlo studied German and collected Yiddish poetry by German writers and read about the persecution of the Jews in Nazi Germany. Her final public appearance was an act of solidarity with Latin American struggle—in her wheelchair, at a march against the U.S. intervention in Guatemala in 1954.

In the first half of the twentieth century, Frida Kahlo lived her life with a very twenty-first-century outlook. Her public persona, with its varied Indigenous blouses, dresses, and jewelry, and the hairstyles of the Mexican peasantry, was a kind of performance art; she lived, let us remember, in an age when tailored wool American suits and European haute couture were favored among the Mexican elite. In this haughty milieu, Kahlo "performed" the complexity of her racial and ethnic identity. Today we know it's possible to live in a Latino family with undeniably European roots, but to also feel a pull toward the indigeneity and Africanness hidden in that family story. Frida Kahlo saw in the rich variety of her origins a kind of wholeness. This is a key element of her appeal with generations of people called "Latino." When we purchase a Frida Kahlo poster, or a refrigerator magnet, we are mimicking her own cultural practice. Today, we people with "Latino" roots construct a sense of our wholeness by assembling our multiethnic ancestors into a mental picture, a canvas where the meeting of our parents and grandparents is depicted. In this work of art, all the secrets and the unknowns of our family histories are finally revealed, and our whole past is seen and celebrated in the vivid colors of an oil painting.

"LATINO" IS A SYNONYM FOR "MIXED." IT DESCRIBES A COLLI- sion and an accommodation between ethnic groups; Indigenous, European, Black. Inside many if not most Latino families there are stories like that of the Smith family, or the Kahlos. There's one inside my mother's family, a story about two "races" of people coming into contact with each other, and about the inequality and lack of opportunity upon which their relationship is based. Like most such stories, it's clouded in secrecy and tinged with shame.

My paternal grandfather grew up alongside his two cousins and their parents in the home in the center of Guatemala City where this story takes place. This home was made of whitewashed, plastered adobe, and I remember visiting it as a boy and as a young man. My grandfather's cousins were two sisters who were fair-skinned, or canche, to use a Guatemalan slang term. Asunción and Elvira Pérez never married, and after their parents died they inherited the family home and lived there for the rest of their lives. They shared the home with a man named Ramón, who was the coffee-colored hue of Guatemala's Indigenous people and about the same age as Asunción and Elvira; like them, he never married and also lived in that house on Avenida Centro América B until he died. I met Ramón many times. He was, in my memory, balding and quiet, with the gentle smile of the unseen. There was something emotionally stunted about him. The Pérez sisters ran a sundry store from their whitewashed adobe house, and he worked there and slept in the same kind of narrow half room that many middle-class Guatemalan families assign to their servants. The story I grew up hearing about him was that he was a street boy who had been adopted by my grandfather's relatives. Asunción and Elvira and Ramón all died more than a decade ago. My thrice-married and now-widowed mother lives in their old home, and on one of my recent visits to Guatemala the subject of Ramón and the two never-married sisters came up; after four decades my mother's sister Imelda finally told me the truth about him.

Ramón was not a rescued street urchin. In fact, he'd been born in that house, the product of an extramarital liaison between the Pérez family servant, an Indigenous woman named Silveria, and some unknown third party. "Ella era de traje," my aunt Imelda tells me of Silveria, meaning she wore the embroidered Indigenous dress of the Maya each and every day. Silveria abandoned her newborn baby boy and left him and returned to her village in the interior of Guatemala and to "her people," keeping from them the secret of her son's birth; baby Ramón was raised and cared for by the Pérez family. But four years later, the story goes, Silveria returned and said she was ready to take care of her son. But the Pérezes said no, and so Ramón stayed with them. He grew up erased of his Indigenous identity, in a home with ladino people, as his Mayan mother might have called them. Until he was an adult, and into middle age, and to his death. He was the child of a passionate, interracial love affair—or of a rape. It seems to me either is as likely. And listening to this story, I realized that this is one of the ways racial mixing has proceeded in Latin America for centuries. Unsanctioned, taboo relationships unfolding in secret spaces. Born of hierarchies and oppression, and sometimes of true affection and shared desires.

"LATINO" AND ITS SYNONYM, "HISPANIC," ARE ETHNIC CATE-gories that are used very often in our society like racial ones; this happens in both casual conversation and in official usage. Media outlets and government agencies use the census category "Hispanic" to create pie charts that give a slice of the demographic pie we share with other groups that are defined as races: "Black," "White," "Asian," and "Native American." Across the United States, police forces describe suspects as "Hispanic males," which can mean a variety of things: a guy who "looks" Mexican or Puerto Rican; a swarthy individual whose clothing and demeanor and dark hair and eyes suggest foreign roots, or proletarian status.

Latino is an inherently mysterious category to the eyes of a person who sees the world through the lens of race. "What *are* you?" is a question I used to get a lot, back in the eighties and nineties, when people were less polite about such things.

What *are* we, indeed? Race-centered thinking causes confusion and unease in our families. We've learned through centuries of practice to be secretive, deceptive, and to presume that we are whiter or better than others. Or that the mixing in our family histories is a kind of character flaw, or a social disability. Long-held taboos have led us to erase our indigeneity, and our Black ancestors, and the many cross-racial couplings that created us.

Gloria Arellanes first became a public figure in Southern California as a Chicana activist. She was a Brown Beret, the 1970s Chicano equivalent of the Black Panthers and the Young Lords. The Brown Berets marched wearing their eponymous headgear, and once paraded with a borrowed army tank through the streets of East Los Angeles, and camped out on Santa Catalina Island and "claimed" it in the name of the Chicano people. They were exponents of Chicano nationalism, and if you had asked Arellanes back then what her ethnicity was, she would have told you Mexican. Her father was fair-skinned, and "could have passed for some kind of Anglo," she would remember. But her mother was "very dark, very brown, very beautiful brown skin, very black hair." Her father, a World War II veteran, moved the family out of her native East Los Angeles and bought a home in a suburban community called El Monte thanks to the GI Bill. Her mother's Native American ancestry was a secret, until one day Gloria fell into conversation with a cousin who had assembled a family genealogy and revealed the truth that they were "Indian." Gloria went home and confronted her mother about this. "What kind of Indian are we?" Gloria demanded.

"You're not Indian," her mother answered. "You are Mexican."

"Well, why does your cousin tell me I'm an Indian?"

"Don't listen to her. You're a Mexican." Gloria's mother slammed the door on her Native past, Gloria would later explain in an oral history recorded by Virginia Espino, "because they were punished for who they were." The Native peoples of California were subjected to violent acts of genocide in the nineteenth century and to discrimination and cultural erasures in the twentieth. Parents hid their Indigenous roots from their children as a protective reflex. But with a bit of digging, Gloria discovered her mother was a member of the Tongva nation, the people who inhabited what is now Los Angeles when the Spanish arrived. Gloria Arellanes, the militant Chicana activist, became a leader in the Tongva nation and a defender of its rights and traditions. From the revealed secret of an intimate family truth, she built a new public identity.

ETHNICITY AND RACE ARE PRESENTED TO US AS FIXED IDEAS with a quasi-scientific basis. But, in fact, they are just names, and they are fluid and malleable. An ethnic and racial identity is born from an encounter of two or more cultures—and the intimacies that are produced by these encounters—and then the identity shifts and evolves, and sometimes it dies. The history of the people now known as "Latino" is filled with stories of "ethnogenesis." Tejano, Californio, Nuevo Mexicano, Boricua, Latinoamericano, Hispanoamericano, and many other terms were created in different parts of the United States from the cross-racial and cross-ethnic intimacies of the people of the Americas, and from their migrations and their desire to reinvent themselves. "A Chicano is a Mexican-American with a non-Anglo image of himself," the journalist Rubén Salazar wrote in 1970, when "Chicano" was an ethnic identifier on the rise. Fifty years later, "Chicano" is fading from use, and is being swallowed up by "Latino" and "Latinx."

The ethnogenesis of "Latino" as a term of pride and self-identification took place in United States cities in the twentieth century as people with roots in different parts of Latin America lived alongside one another and intermarried and fought together in defense of their rights. One scholar pinpoints the earliest contemporary usage of "Latino" to Chicago in the 1970s, where Puerto Rican and Mexican activists formed alliances on employment and housing issues. "Latinx" was born in this century as an expression of solidarity with people questioning gendered identities and the male-female binaries of Spanish grammar. But to some of us the *x* in "Latinx" also stands for the mystery of who we are; it represents the indigeneity, the Blackness, and the mixing hidden inside our secret histories.

ALL RACE AND ETHNIC CATEGORIES BEGIN WITH CRIMES, LIES, distortions, secrets, and myths that gloss over the intimacies of family life. This is true of "Latino" and "Latinx" as much as it is of any other category, if not more so. Even the name "Latino" itself, derived from the term "Latin America," privileges our European ancestors, at the expense of the Indigenous and African people in our family trees.

"Latin America" was coined by nineteenth-century intellectuals eager to spread the notion that the newly independent Spanish-speaking countries of the Western Hemisphere had powerful cultural and emotional ties to "Latin" Europe, and a common foe in Great Britain and English-speaking "Anglo" America. When the French invaded Mexico and installed an emperor loyal to France, French intellectuals proclaimed it an act of "Latin" solidarity. In a similar fashion, the people who coined "Hispanic" and "Latino" were reaching across the Atlantic Ocean to ground our ethnic identity in the lands of the Spanish Crown. But what does it mean to be "Spanish," or to have Spanish roots?

THE CONQUERORS AND COLONISTS WHO ARRIVED IN THE Americas in the sixteenth century did not think of themselves as "Spaniards." Instead, they identified as Castilians, Andalusians, Basques, Gallegos, or any one of the many ethnic identities of the Iberian peninsula. As the historian Ramón A. Gutiérrez tells us in his essay "What's in a Name?" once these multiethnic subjects of the Spanish Crown had settled in North America, they began to call themselves "Spanish" to distinguish themselves from the Native peoples of Mesoamerica and South America, who they called "indios." ("Indian," a racial term derived from a mistake of geography, is arguably the greatest sin ever in the long and shameful history of racial and ethnic naming.) Like "white" and "Black," the creation of "españoles" as a pan-ethnic identity was a response to the creation of new racial hierarchies in the Spanish Americas; "Spanish" expressed a superiority relative to the "Indian."

If we think of racial and ethnic categories as fixed and grounded in history, then we can feel there's something flawed or broken about us if we don't fit inside these labels. Like the young Gloria Arellanes, we feel betrayed when we discover that the categories we have grown up with are based on deception. And yet those categories are, in turn, a powerful presence in our daily lives. We are asked to mark the box "Hispanic" and "Latino" on forms, and most of us carry Spanish surnames; mine is the name of a village in the Burgos region of northern Spain. Many of the most common surnames in the United States are of Spanish origin, with García, Rodríguez, and Martínez all in the top ten alongside Smith, Johnson, and Williams. Spain is one of the foundations of our ethnic identity; we think of it, when we think of it at all, as this distant land that gave the world *Don Quixote*, flamenco, and the alluring eyes of Penélope Cruz. But the travelers who brought our future Spanish surnames with them to the Americas were leaving a place with its own fraught history of racial violence and ethnic conflict.

The same country that sent large numbers of soldiers and settlers to the New World in the sixteenth century was also engaged in a long campaign of ethnic cleansing against Jews and Muslims, who were forced to convert or face expulsion from Spain. Many Jews converted and became "New Catholics." In chapter nine of *Don Quixote*, the narrator encounters Arabic and Hebrew speakers in the marketplace in Toledo, a Spanish city where you can still see the places where Jews and Muslims worshipped. (Miguel de Cervantes, the author of *Don Quixote*, may have been a "hidden Jew.") New Catholics rose to prominent positions in Spanish society, and their growing numbers caused a backlash against "hidden Jews." In one of the earliest examples of race-thinking, Catholic authorities argued that Jewishness, as a legal status, could be passed down through the blood, and that the bodies of New Catholics carried non-Catholic loyalties. The Spanish Inquisition placed suspected Jews on trial in the name of blood purity, and its tribunals gazed into the intimate family practices of New Catholic families. Was no smoke drifting up from their chimneys on Saturday, the day of the Jewish sabbath? Did they order meat from a butcher who was a hidden Jew? The tribunals used such "evidence" to convict suspected Jews and pronounce sentences on them, and burned many alive as large crowds watched.

In other words, if you are a member of that group of people called "Latino," you have a five-century history of cross-racial family intimacies that have been criminalized and shrouded in shame and secrecy. "Latino" and "Latinx" are synonyms for "mixed," and also for "hidden." Life is a telenovela for us now, in our Florida condos, in our New Jersey apartments, and in our Texas subdivisions; a melodrama of love affairs between rich and poor, dark and light, Dominican and white and Black and Mexican, privileged and unprivileged. And it was a telenovela for our ancestors in the towns of New Spain where colonists from Sevilla and Madrid fathered children with their "Indian" servants, and in the Caribbean plantations where the first "mulatos" were born, and in the Andalusian cities where our Jewish ancestors lit candles as a defiant expression of their criminalized faith.

ONE OF THE QUALITIES OF BEING "LATINO" IS THAT YOU EVENtually come to feel the tortured and strange history of the "Latino" past at work inside you, shaping your understanding of the world. You somehow assimilate this knowledge, even if you never go to college, or graduate from high school, or learn to read and write. Our sense of ourselves as characters in an ongoing melodrama expresses itself in our wariness to certain kinds of situations, in our melancholia, in a tendency to value family ties, and many other ineffable qualities that are often called "spiritual." Over the course of many centuries, the emotional and physical violence that created our ethnic and racial and caste identities ("Indian," "peon," "bracero," "undocumented") have left their mark on our way of being, our conception of what our humanity is and might be. We feel wounded or not whole, so we begin asking questions of our relatives, and we assemble genealogies and read books. Or sometimes we simply take a moment at the Thanksgiving table, or at a Christmas gathering, or at a baptism party, to look at the people around us, to listen to them, to take in the shapes of their faces and their eyes and noses, and the sounds of their voices, and to wonder: Where did we come from? And what, exactly, did we suffer deep in a history unknown and invisible to me?

Latino people construct their understandings of themselves is all sorts of roundabout ways. One of my students describes her mother's obsession with the 1948 Mexican film *Angelitos negros*, a tale of a fair-skinned woman with a Black mother in her hidden past, because this story echoed the race secrets and the colorism in her own family. Or we might have an accidental encounter with an old friend, or a conversation with a sibling or a cousin that brings a distant memory into sharper focus. When I was an adolescent, I listened to my father recount the events leading up to the 1954 coup in Guatemala, and his memory of the bombs that fell in Guatemala when he was thirteen years old, and this helped me understand where my family fit in the history of the world. At about the same time, I was absorbing lessons about race-thinking from my American television set. I heard about a country where ancient "race" hatreds gave birth to a system of industrialized mass murder. This was the same, faraway European horror story that worried Frida Kahlo as she scanned the newspapers in her Mexico City studio in 1933 and 1941, and the same one just about every American grows up learning about in the twenty-first century.

8

ASHES

Today, lesson plans about the Holocaust are included in the curricula of most public and private schools in the United States. This was not so when I was going to school in California in the 1970s. My first memories of learning about the genocide committed against the Jews of Europe date to the years of my father's second marriage, when he lived in a Hollywood apartment with a new color television that we turned on every Sunday to watch films in black-and-white. One afternoon, when I was eleven years old, the screen flickered with the surreal images of human beings emaciated by starvation, of bodies stacked in piles, footage shot by Allied troops when they liberated the Bergen-Belsen concentration camp. Not long afterward, my father's third marriage linked me to a Jewish family. I sat at a dinner table with my new step-grandfather, a Russian-born obstetrician who had served in the U.S. Army in Europe, and listened as my new stepmother spoke of relatives who had been killed by the Nazis. In the years that followed, Holocaust dramas began to appear on U.S. television. When I reached my twenties, I read Primo Levi's memoirs of survival and rescue from Auschwitz, and I sat in a San Francisco theater for one afternoon and evening, watching all nine hours of Claude Lanzmann's landmark documentary *Shoah*, including its interview with the Jewish barber forced to trim the hair of his compatriots inside a gas chamber. When I wrote my first novel, *The Tattooed Soldier*, which was set against the backdrop of the mass murder perpetuated against the Maya in Guatemala, I read Robert Jay Lifton's study of the psychology of the perpetrators of genocide, *The Nazi Doctors*.

Over the years, I've met a handful of other Latino people who share this obsession (most of whom don't have Jewish family). The reason why we would be drawn to these events is both obvious to me and a source of mystery. The Holocaust against the Jews in Europe in the 1930s and '40s isn't the only mass killing perpetuated against a "race" of outsiders, but it is the best-documented and the most accessible to the average American. From Anne Frank's *The Diary of a Young Girl* and the writings of Elie Wiesel, to *Schindler's List* and *The Pianist*, Holocaust narratives have served to underpin the cultural values of the United States in the half century after the passage of the Civil Rights Act: the idea that American democracy must embrace racial and ethnic tolerance, and turn its back on ideologies of race hatred and violent extremism. We understand that when we look at the Holocaust we are seeing the pools of blood, the barbed wire, and the piles of ordure that rest beneath the foundations of "Western civilization."

When I was seventeen, my Holocaust obsession collided with the carnage of the Central American present. I sat in a darkened campus lecture hall and watched *Rev-*

olución o muerte, a documentary about the Salvadoran Civil War. The screen before me filled with real-life scenes, filmed less than a year earlier, in which soldiers massacred scores of people outside San Salvador's cathedral and on the campus of El Salvador's national university. I saw bodies of protesters pierced by bullets, and a student of about twenty, calling out to his comrades to be brave, and then writhing in pain and weeping for his mother as he died from gunshot wounds. Here was a story with the stark scenes of a holocaust, unfolding in my times, and in a country I had visited with my father just a few years earlier. My life direction changed in that moment. In the decades that followed, I found myself returning to the martyred dead of Latin America again and again. I traveled to the indoor arena in Chile where the folk singer Víctor Jara was executed, one of more than two thousand people to die in that country's 1973 military coup. I spoke to Jara's widow, and in Buenos Aires, I interviewed a mother whose kidnapped and "disappeared" son had been held captive in the Escuela Mecánica de la Armada, the notorious torture center where 4,500 people were detained before being murdered by Argentina's military junta.

My novel *The Last Great Road Bum* contains a description of soldiers opening fire on a crowd of marchers, based on an actual event that unfolded in San Salvador in 1979. When my father read this passage he told me a story about an act of violence he witnessed when he was an adolescent in Guatemala City. He was passing by the headquarters of the national police, a castle-like structure in the center of the city, when he saw a small group of mothers protesting to demand the police release their sons and daughters. Suddenly, an officer raised a gun and began firing at the women. My father ran away, terrified, and could not see if anyone had been hit, but he was left with the memory of a moment when he was in close proximity to death. A few years later, I was born. My father never told me that story growing up—until my novel transported him back to that incident, more than sixty years later. I had to write several books and hundreds of thousands of published words over the course of many decades to tease that memory from my father's brain and out into the shared space of my family history, and to now preserve it in these pages.

Recent science has shown how trauma can change our brain chemistry and our DNA. I wonder now if my lifelong obsession with stories of mass murder is tied to my father's memory of that moment, and others that exposed him to the violence of empire, poverty, and dictatorship in the years before I was born. The brain stores information for its own survival, and it finds a way to pass on its lessons from generation to generation. Perhaps my curiosity about organized, official violence is a biological signal sent by the survivors and the perpetrators of atrocities from a distant and unwritten history. From the Spanish Inquisition, the Middle Passage, the conquest of the Americas. Unremembered for many generations, those horrors may still be alive, in me, and in many people like me, in our instinctual desire to stare into, and to understand, the dark and bloody recesses of human history.

TODAY, THE HORROR OF MASS DEATH CLOSEST TO THE DAILY lives of the American people unfolds at the Mexican border. Every year, several hundred or a thousand people or more die while trying to cross the deserts and scrublands of the Southwest. They come from across the Americas: Guatemala, Honduras, Colombia, Ecuador, and other countries. Many are men and women and children seeking to be reunited with their families in the United States. Most perish crossing the Sonoran Desert, where flame and fire are the metaphors used to describe the unrelenting heat. The desert is a furnace, it is "el camino del diablo."

The government officials who created the physical and technological barriers at the Mexican border knew that they would be funneling migrants into deserts that would be deadly to cross; in a 1997 report of the Government Accountability Office, a bureaucrat hypothesized that an increase in "deaths of aliens attempting entry" would be one measure of success of the program the Border Patrol called "Prevention Through Deterrence." In Arizona and California, the U.S. government created, as the anthropologist Jason De León puts it, "a killing machine that simultaneously uses and hides behind the viciousness of the Sonoran Desert." In this remote and inhospitable corner of North America, the bodies of the immigrant dead are slowly being transformed into bonemeal.

The United States Border Patrol reported more than eight thousand deaths of migrants crossing the southwestern border between 1998 and 2019, but observers of the border believe that the number is underreported by a factor of between two and ten. In 2012, De León and a group of scientists conducted an experiment that illustrated the process by which the immigrant dead are erased from the landscape. They killed several pigs (an animal used often in forensic studies for its anatomical similarities to human beings), dressed them in the clothes and underwear of men and women, and left them in various positions under a summer sun, with cameras nearby to monitor them. Ants and flies began the first stages of decomposition, then dogs approached the corpses, while turkey vultures hovered nearby. After waiting five days, the vultures began to peck and pull at the flesh of the animals, pulling out intestines, and cracking open the skulls to reach brain matter. The vultures eventually ripped away the limbs of the pigs and carried them off. After nine days, the bodies were almost completely dismembered, with the remaining bones scattered over an area the size of a baseball diamond. The study had found, as De León put it, that nature was performing acts of desecration upon the dead.

One of the final creatures to feed upon the corpses of those who die in the desert is the hide beetle, which specializes in eating dried, hard tissue. If and when a forensic examiner finds and examines remains, these beetles will often remain with the corpse in the bag used to transport it to the morgue. During an especially horrible summer in Pima County, Arizona, one of these medical examiners told an interviewer that "we're just crushed by the weight of all the dead and all the missing persons reports . . . It's like working a mass disaster when people are still dying and planes are still crashing around you. And you, you throw your hands up in the air sometimes and you just think, when's it gonna stop?" The work of De León and others shows how a body can all but disappear in little more than a month. When De León traveled to a site where fragments of a human corpse were discovered, he found a piece of bone the size of a fingernail and squeezed it; it turned to dust.

The Sonoran sun and its wind and animals and insects

are slowly eliminating the evidence of a mass killing. By forcing migrants into the desert, the United States government has, in effect, subcontracted acts of violence and erasure both from the criminal syndicates of northern Mexico and from nature. In his book *The Land of Open Graves: Living and Dying on the Migrant Trail*, De León quotes a newspaper reader who suggested that the U.S. government "take some of those dried out corpses" and "hang them at the places where they [migrants] are known to cross." But the genius of the U.S. policy is that it makes such overt acts of intimidation unnecessary. The mass killing at the southwestern border is achieved through passive means, and in this fashion it perfectly fits the modern American character. The desert is a natural machinery of death set in motion by policy makers who can deny trying to kill anyone, or who can shift the blame to the dead themselves. The deaths at the border serve the same function as a public execution: untold numbers of potential immigrants are dissuaded from undertaking the journey, and in the United States the sense among Latino people that we are a lesser, beaten-down caste is deepened. In this fashion, the ultimate goal of U.S. immigration policy is achieved now as in the twentieth and nineteenth centuries: the preservation and protection of the "white" character of the United States. All the while, the corpses are disposed of in a region that's far from the nation's major media markets, slowly and silently, and without spectacle. In this country, nothing really exists unless there's a video of it. If you were to try to invent a perfect American slaughter for the media age, it would happen in this way.

––––––

WITH THE BOSNIAN WAR AND THE MASSACRE AT SREBRENICA and the siege of Sarajevo, and with the Rwandan genocide and its mass murders by machete and fire, the Holocaust followed me from my childhood into the future. And I have followed the Holocaust back in time, with a reading of the history of the Armenian genocide and the mass deportations of Native American people in the nineteenth-century United States. I now understand that all of these events are deeply interconnected. In his book *Unworthy Republic: The Dispossession of Native Americans and the Road to Indian Territory*, the historian Claudio Saunt argues that the 1830 expulsion of Indigenous peoples from the lands east of the Mississippi inspired European nationalists to conduct similarly cold-blooded ethnic removals in Algeria, Poland, and elsewhere; they believed the extermination of the Native peoples of North America was the basis of the triumph of the United States as an economic power. The Nazis were inspired by both the Armenian and the Native American genocides; Eastern Europe was to be the frontier where they gained "living space" at the expense of the Slavs who lived there. And today I can read about the Chinese thinkers who say their government's campaigns against the Uyghur and Tibetan peoples will create a monocultural "state-race" that will make China "a new type of superpower." Modern societies use race and ethnicity to create the social discipline to build empires, and to defend "nationhood" and nationalist projects, or to preserve the illusion of empire in an age of decadence. Ethnic hatreds and race engineering are the dark force that created the modern world, and we are still living with the pathologies, the lies, and the horrors and the habits of that history.

All race crimes share a genealogy, including the suffering, the ritual humiliations, and the death inflicted upon Latin American immigrants in the United States of our times. As "Latino" people, as those descended from slaves and peons, we must see our histories, and our emotional and political selves, within the continuum of this history.

WHEN I LEARNED ABOUT THE BODIES OF LATIN AMERICAN immigrants being turned into bonemeal in the desert, I remembered the story of Michael Goldman-Gilad, a Polish teenager who ended up in Auschwitz. In the final months of World War II, he escaped from one of the Nazis' infamous death marches, and joined a band of Soviet partisans. He made his way to Israel and became a police investigator; in 1960 he was one of the officers supervising the detention of Adolf Eichmann, the SS officer who was one of the principal organizers of the bureaucracy that sent millions of Jews to their deaths. When the Israeli government put Eichmann on trial, Goldman-Gilad was there; he witnessed Eichmann's execution and cremation, too, and saw the ashes of the dead man fill a two-liter milk jar. The sight of Eichmann's ashes transported Goldman-Gilad back to Auschwitz, and to the day when the SS men running the camp ordered him to take shovelfuls of ash from a mountain near the ovens where the bodies of murdered Jews were cremated; he was to spread them on the icy paths of the camp so the guards would not slip. Looking at the small container with Eichmann's ashes, Goldman-Gilad realized, for the first time, that the huge pile of ashes at Auschwitz contained the remains of hundreds of thousands of people.

It's a common tendency among the perpetrators of

mass violence to attempt to erase the evidence of their crimes, and to shield their own people from the horrors they inflict on others. The Nazis created an industrial death machine and transformed their victims into ashes, in part, to spare German soldiers and policemen the life-altering trauma of looking into the eyes of their victims as they killed them, and to keep the crime secret, in a failed attempt to distance the German people from the stigma of the murder of millions of people. The Argentine junta kidnapped people from their homes, or off the street, and then claimed to know nothing about their whereabouts, spinning the fiction that they had "disappeared." Later, they would drug their victims into sleep, and drop them from airplanes into the vast waters of the Río de la Plata estuary, never to be found; in this fashion, they exterminated a large portion of the young Argentine intelligentsia. Soldiers of the Ottoman Empire marched Armenian families out into the Syrian Desert, where they died of starvation and exposure to the elements, far from the sight of their Turkish neighbors, and where their bones were often left to bleach and crumble in the harsh desert air. The regimes that launch campaigns of mass violence and intimidation also burn documents, and they seal off the camps and the detention centers where they concentrate and punish their victims. And they locate those camps in remote wastelands, amid dust and desert flora, as the United States government did in the Japanese internment.

The perpetrators of such violence know that many if not most of the people in whose name they commit these acts of aggression will find them morally distasteful, and that revealing the cruel and sadistic nature of those crimes would subtract from the legitimacy of their regimes and their movements. This is the tension at the core of any project that uses violence and intimidation to achieve goals of social engineering: to employ enough force and cruelty to cast fear into the outsider, or to marginalize or expel the outsider from a society—while at the same time trying to convey a sense of order and normality to the people in whose names these acts are carried out.

The United States of our time is at odds over how much cruelty it should direct toward Latin American immigrants. Only a small minority of Americans protest the daily hurt and indignities inflicted on immigrant families: a teenage girl's screams when her father is detained by ICE as he is about to drop her off at school, or the ankle bracelets that immigrant mothers are forced to wear after they are released from detention. The United States government can shame and wound Latino people in this way and say it is necessary for the preservation of order and the "rule of law." When a doctor performs unnecessary, nonconsensual hysterectomies on women in immigration detention, or when a seven-year-old girl dies in immigration custody, the government convinces most Americans that these are isolated incidents. But when the president of the United States decided, in 2017, to intimidate Latino immigrants with a "zero tolerance" policy that separated children from their parents, and when his government gathered those children in cages, most Americans recoiled in disgust. They listened to the recording of the children wailing inside a warehouse transformed into a concentration camp, heard the stories of detained children in diapers being cared for by other detained children, and of toddlers sleeping on floors with foil sheets as blankets. For a few news cycles, the barbarism of United States immigration policy was plain to see.

Across the political spectrum, elected officials and pundits declared: This is not who we are, as a people. Americans should not do these things.

Our daily comfort, the cleanliness of our cities, and the very food we eat are the product of a social discipline built from fences, cages, barbed wire, and mass detention. The taut bounce in the sheets of a bed made by a centroamericana housekeeper and the sturdy frame of a home newly built by mestizo hands are linked to mass death and suffering in a desert wasteland. The peace and prosperity of the United States rests upon the foundations of a million crossings of this desert purgatory—and also upon the slaughter at a San Salvador cathedral, and the tortures and disappearances ordered by clownish dictators who proudly declared themselves to be "friends of the American people." The challenge of the protectors of the race-order of the United States is to erase this history of violence and to make the cruel excesses of the present seem abnormal, distant. They must shrink the offense and its epic scale into inconsequential, isolated "tragedies," so that the American people can believe themselves to be good and decent human beings. So that the images of caged infants do not enter their dreams.

FROM THE VERY BEGINNINGS OF UNITED STATES HISTORY, THE violence required to maintain the unequal, race-centered social order of the United States has transformed the people in whose name those acts are carried out. Put another way, acts of genocide, enslavement, and exploitation eat away at their perpetrators and enter their collective subconscious. In her book on the Salem witchcraft crisis of 1692, the historian Mary Beth Norton argues that the mass unreason of that time and place was sparked, in part, by the horrors witnessed by families of white settlers in their war with Native American tribes in the nearby Maine frontier. The girls of Salem were raised to think of the Native people as devils, and then they saw the devil in their white neighbors. In our times, deranged men fire assault rifles indiscriminately at their fellow human beings in public places. They arm themselves with weapons that were invented, in part, as instruments of colonial subjugation, and they use them to create a spectacle in which they reenact the massacres of empire building, the genocides that created the modern world. Yesterday, a Native American or a Vietnamese village; today, a mall, a concert, or a school.

Over the course of many centuries, the crimes of race and empire have slowly eroded the moral fabric upon which the ideas of "white" and the "United States of America" were constructed. The same attitude that leads people to shrug their shoulders at the incarceration of Latino children, or the sight of immigrant corpses piled in the back of a truck, leads them to turn away from the mass disaster of homelessness in U.S. cities, and from the crises of addiction in rural communities. The creation of a laboring caste of "brown" people is further deepening the numbing of the American soul.

Unable to come to terms with what is happening to their country, the American people lose themselves in odd beliefs. In wacky conspiracy theories and fairy tales about the "simple" and dangerous folk who have come to live among them.

9

LIES

To be Latino in the United States is to see yourself portrayed, again and again, as an intellectually and physically diminished subject in stories told by others. Very often, these are tales shared by people who are entirely sympathetic with our "plight." As with the well-meaning, principled North American activist whose words enter my orbit via a mass email. She is part of a team of volunteers whose mission is to help immigrants released from ICE detention. "Our work provides a little outpost of refuge and kindness for those who happen to be traveling north via Greyhound, running from despair toward hope for a better life here," the activist writes. She describes the degraded and pathetic state of the migrants she encounters at a bus station in Texas: the ICE-issued sacks in which they carry their belongings, their state of confusion, and how utterly innocent they are when faced with the simple facts of United States geography, such as the many days it will take to travel from Texas to New York. The immigrants don't speak in her account. The protagonist of the story is the activist herself; the email is a description of the routine of her daily actions in support of the immigrants, and the drive she feels to get up each morning to pass out sandwiches, maps, and water bottles. The immigrants have "bewildered brown faces," and there is nothing to distinguish one from the other. "There is no time to ask or learn anyone's names," she writes, which strikes me as doubtful; she's in a bus station in a metropolis one hundred and fifty miles from the border, and there are no ICE agents on the heels of the migrants, all of whom have been released on their own recognizance. They are not, at that point, "running" from anyone. One imagines that at least some of the migrants were waiting at the station for the next bus to Houston, New Orleans, or Chicago for half an hour or an hour, or longer, and that the activist might have had time not only to learn their names but also to hear them tell a funny or uplifting story. The migrants remain unnamed in her account because their names don't serve the purpose of her story. It is isn't about them; it's about her. The migrants are brown extras with bewildered faces in a tale meant to illustrate the activist's selflessness and compassion.

I read these words and feel insulted and impotent. The social conventions of the milieu in which I am living prevent me from firing back a mass-email response to the activist's clichéd account of the immigrant experience. Doing so would mark me in my professional circle as a cynical malcontent, and an ingrate. The writer of the letter is, after all, helping "our people." Despite her vanity, she is an ally, doing undeniably important work. So I don't say anything at all. This is a common response among Latino professionals. We see our people infantilized in one narrative after another, and we do little or nothing. We've allowed the toxic lie that our people are powerless and naive and backward and guileless to persist and strengthen its grip on United States society. Now the lie follows us around everywhere. It's why a barista at my local Starbucks thought they could write "beaner" on a customer's cup and get away with it. It's why our brightest students are discouraged by their high school "counselors" from applying to the best universities. Now the lie of the stereotyped image of the passive, helpless Latino lives inside the trick mirror in our bedrooms and bathrooms: we look at our reflected image and in our darker moments we see this weak and inconsequential person, this victim. And we say, this is how we are, how I am.

STORIES ABOUT LATINOS, AND ABOUT IMMIGRANT PEOPLE, have become weapons in an ongoing political struggle. Each newspaper story, blog post, or photo essay is a potential tool, an argument in defense of our humanity. Authors and activists make the immigrants in do-gooder narratives, in television news accounts and magazine features, helpless because the argument of the story demands that they be helpless. When a people are in a battle for their survival, the practical thing to do is to make each representative of that agony into a perfect package of suffering. So Latino people are battered and abused in the media again and again. The media transports Latino immigrants into an electronic purgatory of perpetual misery. They are "running" even when no one is chasing them; and "in the shadows" even when they're standing in the bright light of a United States day. The activists, the journalists, and the fiction writers of pro-immigrant narratives imagine a skeptical white audience judging the actions of the Latino characters in their emails and their manuscripts. So they decide to ignore the complications, and the shades of gray that are plain to see when you look at the full, unadorned truth of any human life. Why give the enemy ammunition for their hateful arguments? When my novel *The Barbarian Nurseries* was published, with its prickly and surly Mexican (and undocumented) housekeeper as its protagonist, a respected Latinx book critic asked me: "Aren't you worried about introducing an unsympathetic character into the immigration debate?"

In journalism and nonfiction narratives especially, our Latino protagonists are as pure in heart and conduct as the martyrs in a Sunday-school story. This spirit infects a great deal of Latinx artistic production, as well, and is even more present in works about us written by sympathetic white artists. Literature and theater and television about the Latino experience is replete with didactic narratives that illustrate the basic outline of our history at a grade-school level; these works tell stories of our "nobility," and of racists and our victimized bodies, all written by artists who push at the open door of white guilt. The border wall, and the policies of mass expulsion and detention, the drama of "immigration policy," all contribute to infantilizing Latino people in American media. We cannot be our true selves on the page, and on the screen and on the stage, as long as this human disaster hangs over our people. Or so it seems.

IN THE BEST LITERATURE ABOUT THE IMMIGRANT EXPERIENCE, our unadorned and complicated humanity is presented in all its fullness. My favorites include Reyna Grande's excellent memoir *The Distance Between Us*, with its deeply scarred, emotionally abusive father and love-starved mother; Obed Silva's searing account of his father's alcoholism, *The Death of My Father the Pope*; and the poetry of Marcelo Hernandez Castillo and Javier Zamora, with their stories of closeted sexuality, a grandfather wielding a machete against his family, and a mysterious, sensitive gang member who befriends a border crosser. Aaron Bobrow-Strain's *The Death and Life of Aida Hernandez* tells the story of an everywoman from a U.S.-Mexico border town who falls in love with an Ecuadoran woman—when they're both inside an immigrant detention center. Bobrow-Strain presents the Kafkaesque elements of Aida's detention as but one chapter in a longer story of Aida's border community and her family, an epic that's also about the rise and decline of mining in Douglas, Arizona, her father's membership in a doomed guerrilla army in Mexico, her pregnancy at age sixteen, her encounters with violent Latino men, and her struggles to contain the self-hate and the rage that have welled up inside her.

When an immigrant like Aida appears at the exit of a detention center in a liberal activist's writing, she is divested of her history and its human messiness; her charm and the barbs of her personality are erased. She was never a teen mother, and she has no lesbian lover, no sexuality, and no rage. Most often, she doesn't even have a name.

THE IMMIGRANTS IN RIGHT-WING CONSPIRACY THEORIES ARE nameless too, and completely stripped of humanity. They are a dangerous, infected mass, described with metaphors from nature: they are a wave, a herd, a virus, a disease.

More than a dozen years ago, when I was still a scribe for a daily newspaper, another email reached me. This one had been crafted by a hater of Latino immigrants, and it had been circulated by many other haters. It purported to detail, with a list of ten "facts," the calamity Latin American immigrants were inflicting on the state of California. Filling up its prisons, hospitals, and public housing—and taking over the airwaves with Spanish broadcasts. Nearly all the "facts" on the list were twisted manipulations of actual statistics, or the paranoid musings of conservative commentators. One item on the list cited a government report available on the internet—which turned out to be a total fabrication. The government agency cited in the report did not exist on the date when the report was supposedly authored. An anonymous nativist had crafted this document as part of a deliberate campaign of ethnic slander against Latino people.

I was reminded of *The Protocols of the Elders of Zion*, an early twentieth-century text that purported to be the minutes of a meeting of Jewish leaders who were plotting to take over the world. The *Protocols* were penned by Russian anti-Semites and exposed as a fraud not long after they first appeared in print. But millions of people continued to read them and believed them to be real. Conspiracy theories about Jews blamed them for most of the ills facing the Russian, German, English, and finally the American people in the nineteenth and twentieth centuries, and continue to do so to this day. Anti-Semites have blamed the Jews for the rapaciousness of Western capitalism, and for communist revolutions and Marxist regimes. And today, a small but persistent group of conspiracy theorists blames them for flooding the United States with "illegal immigrants" as part of a plot to advance Jewish world domination.

In the darkest strands of conspiracy theories associated with Latin American immigration, the migrants themselves are pawns being controlled by larger powers. Central American families trudge down a Mexican highway in a picture shared in a social media post, illustrating a caption that suggests they are hirelings of George Soros, a Hungarian-born financier who also happens to be Jewish. They have been "sent by Soros," who has "manufactured" the crisis from which they are fleeing. A Republican member of Congress shares a video of migrants receiving small sums of cash and asks, in a tweet, "Soros?" In all these posts, the Latino immigrants are sheep heading stupidly northward to the United States, where they will become "Democratic voters" and public charges. In 2018, one follower of these conspiracy theories blamed a Jewish refugee organization for funding the caravan of Central Americans walking through Mexico to the United States. He later entered a synagogue in Pittsburgh and murdered eleven people. Some months later, another man, a follower of the "Great Replacement" conspiracy theory (the idea that migration by people of color is part of a plot to eliminate "white" society) entered a big-box retailer in El Paso and killed twenty-three people.

In the minds of murderers, and of law-abiding conservatives who spread misinformation as they go about their daily chores, Latino immigrants are a mob of passive and unintelligent people, divested of individual desires. Or we are "invaders" killing white people, displacing them from their American homeland. Latino immigrants are not human beings to these white people, but abstractions. We have become actors inside the darker corners of the collective white subconscious, symbolic representations of the inner torments of people who are angry and adrift. They see their world spiraling into chaos and they believe they have found an explanation—us.

THE GREAT IRONY OF THE CONSPIRACY THEORIES IS THAT Latino people are, in reality, working to keep the order and efficiency of American society intact, to keep the machine of American middle- and upper-class life running smoothly. As I write these pages, a team of Spanish-speaking workers delivers a refrigerator to my home, and then other appliances to other homes, twenty or more in a single day, they tell me. A Mexican American tow-truck driver clears a broken-down car from the street in front of my home, and then goes on to rescue many other vehicles. Down the road, there is a golf course where I once met the gardeners and maintenance men, all members of an extended Mexican family—and excellent golfers. "You have to keep your head down," one yelled at me from across the fairway. "That's why you're slicing the ball." Across America, the roads stay clear, and the milk and the butter stay cooled, and the greens trimmed, thanks to Latino labor.

And yet, the most common representation of Latino people in television and film is as agents of chaos. Latino male actors get work playing the hitmen, bosses, and victims of Latin American crime syndicates. In the television series *Breaking Bad*, the high school chemistry teacher Walter White becomes a producer of crystal meth, a decision that takes him into a brown world of criminals and killers, tattooed and untattooed. He is dying of cancer and is repeatedly demeaned and emasculated at work and at home. We learn that he's been cheated out of his intellectual legacy and financial inheritance by greedy biotech capitalists. With crystal meth, he enters an inverted world where Latinos control everything and the rule of the strongest applies; where brown men carry automatic weapons and train their dogs to fight; a world so immersed in crude Latinidad, that even the white guys he encounters there say things like "hey, ese" and "vato loco gotta make a living." To survive in this world, Walter White must learn to kill Latino people; in *Breaking Bad*, as in all cartel dramas, white protagonists reenact the bloodletting of empire. They defeat Latino rivals and annihilate dark-skinned Natives, proving to themselves, once again, that white people really are smarter and stronger.

Cartel dramas are allegories about the powerlessness of white people in late-capitalist America. In *Breaking Bad*, Walter White is victimized by living in a society where ever-more hours of work and ever-larger sums of cash are needed to survive (among other things, he has a six-figure medical bill). The protagonist of Clint Eastwood's film *The Mule* is an elderly man who is so consumed by his professional ambitions that he misses his daughter's wedding; when his business collapses, he finds new work delivering drugs to the Midwest for a Mexican cartel. In real life, economic devastation has spread across the Midwest, and other corners of the United States, thanks to globalization and the flight of industrial capital to the Global South. In *The Mule*, the voracious and cynical ethos of capitalism is represented by the brown-skinned hyper-entrepreneurs of the cartels. In most movies of this genre, the scriptwriters (white men, usually) create their imaginary cartel organizations from another reality with which they are intimately familiar: corporate America and the decadence and brokenness it has engendered. Hollywood's cartels are demented corporations on steroids, Mexicanized versions of Wall Street. The bad guys in cartel dramas spend lavishly—scenes of sicarios sipping tequila poolside, with their arms wrapped around brown beauties in bikinis, are de rigueur in the genre. They also pursue profits at all costs, seek to crush their rivals, and keep a firm grip on their employees. "We own your ass," a Mexican American cartel lackey tells Clint Eastwood's elderly protagonist, waving a weapon in his face and showing him a corpse in a trunk. In *The Mule* tattooed Latinos are symbols of a white man's powerlessness; Mexican prostitutes symbolize his unchecked desires.

Horror films take something familiar and safe, and transform it into something deadly and lethal: an old home, a flock of birds, a man in a clown suit. The cartel movie operates on the same principle. Most Americans know and interact with Latino people in their daily lives. The cartel genre sends the message that there is something dangerous and villainous lurking beneath the seemingly friendly and benign exterior of their Latino coworkers and neighbors. The protagonist of *The Mule* is introduced to the cartels by a Mexican American guy he meets at his granddaughter's prewedding reception. In the hateful, widely panned film *Peppermint*, an American woman takes on Latino drug dealers whose operations are based in a piñata factory. The dialogue and imagery of cartel movies associate Latino identity with inherent, "pure" evil again and again. "We're dealing with a virus," a Mexican cop tells his U.S. counterpart, describing the drug-fueled corruption overwhelming a fictitious Mexican town in the television drama *SEAL Team*. "Here, everyone is born infected."

The cartel villain is the negative image of the other

dominant trope of the Latinos in United States film and television: the inconsequential immigrant. The "Mexican" or South American who is a nonthreatening, passive, uneducated Juan or María in the background of dramas and comedies about white people. In these works we are silent witnesses to white pathos. We see white tears, we watch white people destroy their marriages and their hotel rooms. Our presence adds a moral weight to the events we are witnessing. Or a sense of absurdity, as in Quentin Tarantino's *Pulp Fiction*, in which an armed Tim Roth takes over a diner and yells, "Mexicans, out of the fucking kitchen!" Or we are the butt of jokes, as in Tarantino's *Once upon a Time in . . . Hollywood*, in which Brad Pitt tells a weepy Leonardo DiCaprio, "Don't cry in front of the Mexicans," as a pair of red-vested parking-lot valets stand nearby.

Hollywood will continue to make us into villains and nonentities until there is a seismic shift in the social and cultural perspectives in American society, akin to the one Black people brought forth in the decades after the passage of the 1964 Civil Rights Act. When that day comes, Latinx people will get "in the face" of this country's cultural barons inside their boardrooms and their living rooms. And there will be hundreds upon thousands of Latino people marching on the streets demanding much more than mere "equity" and respect on the screen. When we are marching often and persistently, demanding immigration reform and housing reform and education reform. When the spirit of protest infects our own homes, when it becomes the daily subject at our dinner tables. That is when we will shift the politics of "representation" in this country. When the Hollywood mogul or director comes to fear the uppity attitude of his Latinx maid or driver. When their racist and offensive and paternalistic depictions of us become taboo because we have exposed them, again and again, as the clichés and lies that they are.

ONE OF THE FEW TIMES I ACTUALLY SPOKE UP AGAINST LATINO clichés—with my spoken voice, in a room, with other people present—came long before I was the settled, home-owning, family-man professional I am today. I was twenty-four, and the editor of a community newspaper. I visited a San Francisco art gallery that a photojournalist and artist had filled with black-and-white images of Mexicans and others being tied up and hustled away by the Border Patrol south of San Diego. This was in the mid-1980s, long before any fence or wall was built there. The detained immigrants had the startled expressions of children caught misbehaving, or confused peasants caught up in a modern legal system they couldn't hope to understand. One handcuffed woman wore a shirt that bore the words HIGH LIFE. The photograph reveled in the irony. I told the photographer I objected to the quantity and monotony of the images, which hit the same pathetic and melodramatic note over and over. To mount them on a wall and call it art was offensive, I told him. Each of his subjects possessed a personality he had failed to capture. "Dude, this isn't who they are," I said. "This isn't who we are."

Three decades later, visuals of immigrant suffering have become the dominant representation of Latino people in United States journalism. We see Latino men and women detained at street corners, locked inside pens, weeping as they say farewell to their children before surrendering to the authorities who will deport them. The relationship between those stark images and the reality of Latino life is analogous to the relationship between pornography and literature. Like pornography, these images are meant to give the viewer dominance over their subjects; they portray brown people who are docile and submissive, aliens to the orderly and affluent rule of white America.

THE IMAGE OF HELPLESS BROWN PEOPLE IN THE STATIC, ONE-dimensional images of immigration porn is a lie. Or at best a half-truth. In the full, four-dimensional truth of lived experience, the man or woman in detention wrestles to defend their humanity; he seeks allies inside the ad hoc cages this country has created for him; and even when she can't avoid a terrible outcome, she finds ways to cheat the system of its ultimate goal, the humiliation and subjugation of herself and her family.

I sit down with Gisel Villagómez and her husband at an outdoor eatery and bar off of Sunset Boulevard in the Silver Lake district of Los Angeles. We are meeting to talk about her experiences as an "essential worker" and DACA recipient during the COVID-19 pandemic. But even before we can order our beers, she begins to tell me about the day she spent in immigration detention, thirteen years earlier. "If you don't mind, if I could describe it . . ."

She was eighteen years old. A year earlier, ICE had come to her home in a community called Huntington Park to arrest her mother and older sister, and Gisel had hidden in the closet with her dog. The family had come to the United States when Gisel was two, with her mother "carrying me in her arms over the border, old school." At some point the family unwittingly hired a con man posing as an attorney, and he filed falsified papers with the immigration authorities on her family's behalf. For this "crime," Gisel's mother and sister were deported to Mexico, and Gisel was left alone to pay the mortgage on her house, which she did, while also enrolling in her local community college. She was taking math, French, and writing classes, and was headed to work one morning when she saw a navy-blue Ford Explorer following her. Agents emerged to stop and handcuff her. Gisel was about to enter a system of public humiliation through which thousands of Latino people pass through each month; here they are shackled and surrender their clothes and their shoes. If they choose to fight deportation they might spend months or years in a system of privately run detention facilities where the cinder block walls and the aggressive rectangularity of the architecture drive home the idea that they are "aliens." Having seen her mother and sister detained and deported a year earlier, Gisel has prepared herself psychologically for this moment. She tells herself: "You know what? I am not going to let this define me. I am going to still be who I am." She approaches the situation like your average entitled American citizen might. With a sense of justice, she says, which is the way she approaches life in general, "because I'm a Libra." After a five-mile drive to downtown Los Angeles, the agents guide her into a detention facility. "As I'm coming in, I greet everyone." Good morning, officer. Good morning, sir. Good morning, ma'am. Unwittingly, she creates an aura of power around herself, so much so, the agents don't search her even though they search all the other people in detention. "But because I was vocal, saying, 'My name is so-and-so,' there was some kind of, like, respect." The other detainees can see she's a fluent English speaker, and soon she is translating their concerns to the officers. "Can you tell them my kids are alone?" And since Gisel hasn't been searched and still has her cell phone, she allows some of the detainees to make urgent phone calls. When she's caught doing this and her phone is confiscated, Gisel begins to remonstrate with the agents. There are people detained with her who "have children who are American citizens," she says. "Even if you think the parents don't have rights, the children do. If something happens to them, you guys are liable." The agents then allow the detainees to make phone calls to arrange for the care of their children. Gisel calls her older sister, "the mastermind," a woman with adult children of her own, and her sister says: "Ask to speak to a judge."

But soon officers are putting her on a bus headed to the border. Gisel describes a scene that sounds to me like the stories refugees told of being herded and transported during the wars and ethnic-cleansing campaigns of the twentieth century: people of varying ages and economic stations thrown together, headed toward an uncertain, life-changing fate. Teenagers, grandparents, a married couple, and "people who have committed actual crimes." As the bus rolls southward, Gisel and another teenage girl find themselves the objects of the attention of some soon-to-be-deported male convicts. "Want to go with us?" "No, our husbands are waiting for us in Mexico," Gisel says, lying. The bus is very close to the border when it stops, suddenly. She hears an agent call out her last name. "Villagómez!" They tell her, "You're going back to L.A." Before she is let off, she turns to the married couple on the bus and tells them, "Don't let this girl be by herself"; they promise to look after the teenager.

When Gisel returns to the Los Angeles detention center, she's told, "We have a supervisor who wants to talk to you." The supervisor is a "super nice guy," she remembers. He tells her, "You don't look like the kind of person who should be in jail. I'm going to let you go."

Gisel has never forgotten that "whole-day ordeal." "They pluck you right out of the middle of your life." She's spent years analyzing the meaning of that day, the messages that were unspoken, a code hidden inside the way she was treated. "They showed me where my place was," she tells me. Before she was detained, and before she was deported, she was making plans to go to college; afterward, she gave up on those dreams. She became a teenager living on her own, working to pay the mortgage of the family home, and then just to survive. Now she can't buy a home, or visit Mexico to see her mother, who she hasn't seen since that morning the agents came to her home. Yes, Gisel has found a way to thrive. A big nonprofit hired her to be a midlevel manager, and she helped her sister run a garment-manufacturing business during the pandemic, producing hundreds of thousands of masks and protective gowns. Now she's about to start a new management job, offered to her by another company. But the questions and images from that day thirteen years ago still linger. Why did the agents subject her to a physical exam when they were about to deport her? She remembers how she fought to preserve her sense of herself. "By the time I left that place, all the officers knew me. 'Hey, Gisel.' I wasn't going to sit back. I was fighting the system. I infiltrated it," she says, and she laughs. (Some years afterward, a group of undocumented immigrants actually did infiltrate a detention center in Florida, working to free the people inside.)

Her day in detention is the fire underneath her. And it is a burden, a lesson. "It gave me an awareness of the limitations this country set for me." When she says this, I realize for the first time that being undocumented is simply a more extravagant and concentrated form of the discrimination and the inequality built into the experience of being brown, mestizo, or Latinx in the United States.

Gisel remembers something her sister, the undocumented mastermind, has told her more than once: "We have to live like it's the last day, every day."

That's what it means to be undocumented; and what it means to be Mexican, and Mexican American, and Puerto Rican, and Latino and Latinx. Sociology, fate, racism, and the law hang over us. We live with a sense of our precarity before the machinery of injustice—but also with the pride and sense of self-worth our families and communities have given us. We are prepared for whatever fucked-up thing the next turn of history will bring us; or for the lucky turns that can come if we just keep living every day like it's our last day. This way of thinking informs the symbolism behind hanging fuzzy dice from your rearview mirror. Keep rolling the dice, and be prepared for whatever the next roll brings you.

ONE DAY, THE DICE ROLLED IN GISELLE'S FAVOR AND THE Obama administration created DACA and Giselle received an "Employment Authorization" card, as did several hundred thousand other people. Latino is a kind of in-between racial and ethnic category (not white, not Black, not Indigenous, but a little bit of some or all those things), and Latino families find themselves in all sorts of in-between legal categories. You can be a "Permanent Resident," or have "Temporary Protected Status," or be an "alien granted suspension of deportation," or be assigned one of dozens of other visa categories and subcategories. You can live in a mixed-status family, like so many Latino families do these days; say, for example, with parents who are undocumented, an older daughter who is a DACA recipient, and younger children who are U.S. citizens. If you're a DACA recipient, you're really still undocumented, in the eyes of the law. You carry an "Employment Authorization" card that must be renewed every six months, but that allows you to get a Social Security number, and a driver's license, though in some states local officials will tag your license with labels such as "limited term," which is a reminder of the tenuousness of your hold on the few rights granted to you. If you need to leave the country for personal or professional reasons, you must apply to the U.S. government for a "parole," as with the DACA recipient from California who traveled to Tokyo to compete in the Olympic Games.

To those forced to carry them, each "alien" category can feel like an official torment, a scarlet letter. The label attached to you is a reminder of the power of the bureaucracy to reach into your life and pluck you from it at any moment. Many of the labels come with renewal requirements, and deadlines, and numbered forms. Even the permanent resident knows he must conduct himself in a saintlier manner than a U.S. citizen, because a serious arrest can make you "deportable." Like the labels of the Spanish casta system, the categories of the U.S. immigration system are a statement about superiority and inferiority and human worth; and like the Nazis' classification of "blood" and "Aryanness" and "Jewishness" in the Nuremberg Laws, they are a statement of the peril represented by an alien "Other." They inflict a slow-burning anguish on the psyche of millions of people, and they are a reminder of the many real-world punishments that can be inflicted upon their bodies. In recent years, our national and state leaders have put much energy into creating new torments for immigrants in general, and for undocumented people in particular. From the "show me your papers law" in Arizona and the arbitrary selection for interrogation by agents at airport checkpoints to which many of my friends have been subjected, to the decision to separate migrant children from their parents, and fill holding cells with adolescents, grade-school children, and toddlers.

United States immigration policy is a performance in which the souls and the bodies of "aliens" are detained and chased across a desert. It can be a made-for-television event, such as those staged by the governors of Texas and Florida, in which they transported immigrants to Democratic strongholds. The audience for these spectacles is the voter-citizen of the United States, and the goal of the performance is to cement the emotional bond between those citizens and the country's political class. The baroque laws of this country's immigration policy, the detention orders, and the military and engineering projects at the border are intended to send a politician's message of power to a people who feel, increasingly, powerless.

The unspoken messages of the immigration-enforcement theater can be encapsulated by the words "undocumented" and "documented." In their everyday lives, United States citizens can suffer through a kind of undocumented status. They are monitored and persecuted by the electronic systems of the consumer economy, and they suffer through the tyranny of its documentation of their behavior. Bad credit scores can deny them housing or a car loan; unpaid bills can land them in bankruptcy proceedings and in Dickensian debt courts, where a judge can send them to jail. Your lack of health insurance can be a fatal form of undocumentation. Identity theft can make you, in effect, undocumented. And the bad documentation of a past arrest, or prison term, or even unpaid parking tickets, can deny you a job, or the safety of a rented home.

It's no accident that the immigration-enforcement spectacle has taken on ever-greater ferocity the more that Americans, and especially white Americans, feel small before the power of data-driven consumer capitalism. Regardless of their politics, the viewer of the immigration spectacle feels a sense of superiority, and of protection relative to the brown subjects they see rounded up and bussed off across the border. As the number of people detained and deported by ICE increases, and as the drama plays out in starker tones in the media, every United States citizen, regardless of race, feels a little more privileged. Given the rampant homelessness and poverty in the United States, this is no small thing. In a social and psychological sense, U.S. citizenship is defined today, increasingly, as the right not to be rounded up arbitrarily, not to fall into the Kafkaesque nightmare to which the undocumented, and many "legal" immigrants, are subjected.

When the white protagonist of the television documentary *Tiger King* was arrested and convicted on animal-cruelty charges, he called the producers on a prison phone and ranted about the injustice with language that suggested he was being treated like an undocumented immigrant. "I am supposed to be in this country!" he shouted. The Tiger King proclaimed that he was no foreigner, but rather an American "born, raised, innocent until proven guilty." Like the undocumented, he had been "stripped of my clothes, my rights, my identity, my dignity."

The biggest deception of the immigration-enforcement spectacle as it unfolds in the United States media is that it places the immigrant alone at the center of the drama. A Mexican, a Colombian, a Guatemalan in an arena, with eyes open wide in fear as blinding klieg lights beam down upon her. In truth, the persecuted and the persecutor, the victim and the bystander, all share a single stage. The undocumented man at the bus station, the compassionate liberal, the xenophobic retiree, the homeless white "nomad," and the Mexican "Dreamer" are members of the same cast, in the same play. Nothing truly makes sense until you see the actors on the same stage, and hear each of them read their lines, together.

MY FRIEND OBED SILVA RECENTLY GOT HIS CITIZENSHIP AFTER a quarter-century odyssey through the criminal justice system and immigration court. He was born in Mexico, raised in the United States, and in the course of his lifetime a series of labels and statuses have been attached to his name: Permanent Resident, gang member, jail inmate, convicted felon, university graduate, deportable Mexican national, college professor. After youth prison camp, jail, hospital rooms, immigration detention, and a final escape from the purgatory of immigration court, he stood before a United States flag and took the oath that made him an "American." A few days after his citizenship ceremony, I heard him ask, "Why did I get all this luck?" Above all, there was the blessing of being the son of a patient mother, a bookworm who stood by him and taught him the beauty of learning; and the good fortune of having his assault-with-a-deadly-weapon case land in the hands of a compassionate prosecutor; and the small break of having a mellow immigration agent for his citizenship interview, a guy who didn't flinch when Obed told him he'd once tried to kill someone. After every knuckleheaded thing he'd done in his life, some guardian angel had appeared to protect him.

Obed Silva wasn't just "lucky"; he was also persistent and hardworking. But Latino identity, and immigrant identity especially, transports us into mystical places where angels follow us and devils persecute us. Our mysticism is a response to the arbitrariness of the systems that lord over us. The patrolled, unequal landscape of a U.S. city. Or living inside an immigration system where the odds are less in your favor than living outside it. If you're undocumented, a jealous coworker, or an abusive ex-husband can call the authorities on you. Or you can simply take a "wrong" turn one morning, and end up in the radar of an especially officious police officer, one whose traffic stop lands you inside immigration detention, and on a bus or plane back to Latin America. You deal with this precariousness by developing a philosophy in which you commend yourself to the Lord each morning, like the undocumented, fiftysomething immigrant father of three I meet in Georgia. "When I leave my house, I feel anything could happen," he tells me. "But I'm tranquilo. And I'll tell you why. I believe in God." He is living his life well, working hard, respecting people. "I don't go against anyone." He's done the best he can do. Faith has prepared him for the bad luck that might come his way. "If one day things go against me, that's how it's going to be."

To be undocumented is to have your actions subjected to the judgments of others—in the public arena of the "immigration debate" and in the growing paperwork of your personal immigration file. You are led to believe that your odds of beating the system will improve dramatically if you live a pristine life of accomplishment and excellence.

If you become the "Dreamer" in the newspaper story—4.0 GPA, war hero, PhD, top of your class—then you will show this country our people are worthy. Undocumented activists fight back explicitly against this idea; they reject the lie of the "Dreamer" label and narrative, the idea that there are perfect and worthy immigrants, and "bad" criminal immigrants. Instead, they point to the arbitrariness of the systems of prejudice and oppression that place us at the mercy of "luck," that force us to pray that our faults won't count against us.

Our fight is to push our imperfect selves onto the American stage. To stand as we are and force the United States to see us as we are. Lo bueno y lo malo, the tragic and the defiant. And all the other states of being human that lie in between.

A MIGRANT MOTHER REACHES A CERTAIN AGE, AND SHE SEES her adult children standing before the power of the United States, taking stock of their position inside the American empire, and the journeys that brought them here. They tell her of books they've read, stories they've picked up from Instagram, and lessons they've learned from the people they've met and the places they've traveled. In the sight of their furrowed brows and the sound of their questioning voices, she feels a sense of satisfaction and relief; her children have, somehow, steeled themselves against the hurt inflicted upon her people. They have not crushed us, she thinks. We will endure.

I MARRIED INTO A FAMILY WITH PROUD MEXICAN ROOTS. I AM the husband of Virginia Espino, who calls herself Chicana;

thanks to her, the aesthetic and the worldview of the Chicano Movement helped shape the way we raised our children. The word "stupid" was taboo in our family because Virginia had heard that word and the lies associated with it turned against her and the Mexican American people with whom she had grown up. We filled our homes with books for our children to read. Our wedding rings were gold bands engraved with a pattern found on Aztec temples. We gave our children names that could be pronounced easily in Spanish, and that honored their Mexican and Guatemalan ancestors. When the opportunity presented itself to move to Latin America, we did so, in large measure because it meant our sons (who were then five and two years old) would learn to read and write in Spanish. Our daughter was born in Argentina, and we moved to Mexico, and as a family we visited Toltec and Zapotec ruins, and performed the cathartic Chicano ritual of climbing the ancient pyramids at Teotihuacán. When we returned to the United States, our children grew up and made friendships that took them into that big mix of peoples Americans call "diversity." Our sons soon brought home girlfriends who were not "Latina," and then our daughter also brought home a girlfriend who was not Latina. And our children still ate tamales at Christmas, and pan dulce all the time, and they had their own adventures with Latinidad, and with brownness and whiteness, stories I'll allow them to keep as theirs, for them to tell one day.

Finally, more than halfway on the journey of my own life, as a parent and as a husband and as a citizen and thinker, I began to understand what the term "Latino" truly meant. I began to see my "place" in this country clearly for the first time, and I could see my family's story inside a complicated, tragic, comic, and confounding history. I began to write this book. And I returned to the places I can call "home," and saw them with clear and enlightened eyes for the first time. I traveled to the country where my family's story begins, and then I took one journey, and then another, and another, across the nation of my birth.

PART II   **OUR JOURNEYS HOME**

10

LIGHT

Wong Kim Ark spent five months in the immigration detention of his day, aboard a ship in San Francisco Bay, in 1895. He had arrived from Hong Kong, on the steamship *Coptic*, as he had many times before, after visiting his family in China. But this time a customs collector stopped him from leaving the ship and setting foot on American soil. Wong showed the official all the papers he possessed testifying to his birth in the United States, at 751 Sacramento Street in San Francisco. This was the era of the Chinese Exclusion Act, and there were many men in the western United States obsessed with erasing the Chinese from American life. A small but growing number of people of Chinese descent in the United States were native-born Americans like Wong; the nativists were looking for a case that challenged their citizenship. So Wong spent a San Francisco summer and autumn confined to the *Coptic*, and then on other ships anchored in the bay. As his lawyer filed suit in federal court to free him, Wong waited. I can see him in my mind's eye, on the deck of those ships, taking in the salty, murky sea air, and the gray light of many overcast

San Francisco mornings. I can see him watching as the water of the bay, which was bluer then than it is today, lapped at the ships' steel hulls. I do not know, and cannot know, if he dreamed in English or in Chinese as the ocean tides lifted and lowered his ship bunk. But I know with certainty that he lived with the anxiety of the personal disaster that loomed over him: deportation from the country he called home.

I am a United States citizen, and so are many of you, thanks to the five months Wong Kim Ark spent confined to steamships in San Francisco Bay—and thanks to the Chinese American mutual aid agencies that paid for his legal defense. A federal judge ordered Wong freed from his shipboard custody on January 3, 1896, but the legal question of whether a son of immigrants like him was a U.S. citizen remained unresolved. Slowly, *United States v. Wong Kim Ark* worked its way to the Supreme Court. On March 28, 1898, the court ruled by a 6–2 majority that Wong, and all U.S.-born children of immigrants, are United States citizens.

As with so many immigrant narratives, Wong's story has been simplified in the media, with key elements erased. Most journalistic accounts say that he returned to China after his legal victory, and that he "disappeared from history," giving his story an air of mystery and melancholy. As always, the truth is more interesting. In the decades that followed his legal victory, Wong traveled repeatedly (and now freely and confidently) between the ports of Hong Kong and San Francisco. His wife bore four of his children in Guangdong province, in the county of Taishan. But he remained a resident of the United States for three more decades, returning to California after each of his ocean journeys to China.

In Chinese there is one word that means both family

and home: 家. Jiā. Like millions of immigrants of the twentieth and twenty-first centuries, Wong lived in a family and home divided by thousands of miles. He was, like so many of us, a man whose sense of wholeness did not fit inside borders. Wong fought for his U.S. citizenship because he needed it to travel freely between Guangdong and San Francisco, the two poles of his family life. His parents had migrated to the United States in the middle of the nineteenth century, a time of great violence and political unrest in Guangdong and China. British and French troops occupied southern China in the imperialist invasions of the Opium Wars, and hundreds of thousands of people were killed in ethnic warfare. Wong could not start a family in San Francisco because its exclusionary immigration laws effectively barred Chinese women from migrating to the United States, and because five years earlier California had passed a law barring marriage between the white and "Mongolian" races. Like their Latin American counterparts in the present, the people of Guangdong endured forced separations from United States relatives that could span decades and generations. But Wong could not return to the land of his parents and provide the life and comfort he hoped for his family. Guangdong was the Central America of its day; a region suffering through war traumas, political instability, and from the ravages of a trade built on drug addiction.

Wong Kim Ark was born in the United States and lived in this country into his sixties; inevitably, Americanness became a part of his being. In the photographs that accompanied his immigration papers in 1895, he wore the traditional Manchu tunic known as a changshan, and his hair was pulled back in the long braid, or queue, then mandatory in China; in later photographs he wore his hair short and sported a Western suit and tie. But Taishan and Guangdong called out to him to the end of his days. The light of "Ong Sing Village," in the "Foot Ow Section" of Taishan, drew him back again and again; those are the places where his four children were born and educated, and they are listed in the documents his Chinese-born son Wong Yook Jim later used in his successful application for his own United States citizenship.

To feel that your being, your happiness, your wholeness, and your love are divided between two distant spots on the globe is an entirely normal condition in the modern world. And it has been for centuries. I say this because if you live inside more than one "national" identity you can feel abnormal, split, and unsettled. Just as we've been sold the falsehood of race difference, we've been sold the lie that national identity is a static and meaningful category, and that national boundaries are fixed and inviolable. National boundaries create our "illegality" and our "otherness." When your family is split between countries you live in a state of anxiety created by the spectacle and bureaucracy of immigration enforcement. We are family people and we long to travel, as Wong Kim Ark did, between the poles of our family's existence. So that we can see our parents and grandparents, our cousins, the village where we were born, the pueblo that is a part of our family story. We line up at the Guatemalan and Mexican consulates in San Francisco and Atlanta to arrange these journeys, and at the Dominican and Peruvian consulates in New York. Like Wong, we seek out notaries, and the official stamps, and financial statements, and birth certificates required of us by the immigration and visa bureaucracies. But many of us cannot undertake or even plan for this journey—we have been excluded from the freedom to travel between the poles of our existence by the same thinking that sought to deny Wong's citizenship. The borders between our families remain fixed, uncrossable, permanent.

The split consciousness of the multinational soul is a creation of the global economy and it has endured throughout its history; from the age of steamships and stamped "special delivery" letters to the age of jet travel and instant messaging and FaceTime.

The laws, the bureaucracies, the ideologies, the fences, and the agents who enforce the immigration laws and patrol the borders of the Global North are more powerful today than they've ever been. We children of the world's diasporas have come to internalize the cruelty of the laws and the social forces that separate us. We feel schizoid, abnormal, distorted. Life was meant to be an oil painting, a landscape depicting an orderly and beautiful family composition—but when we look at our family portrait we see, instead, a canvas slashed open with a knife. Our histories are not depicted on the surface of the painting, but rather in the dark, empty space behind the ripped canvas.

BEFORE WONG KIM ARK RETIRED AND LEFT THE UNITED STATES permanently at the age of sixty-two, he spent only a few scattered years of his life in China. When I returned to Guatemala in my fifties, for a weeklong visit, it brought the sum total of time I've spent in that country (the place where most of my extended family still lives) to about six months.

Wong's port of entry into China was Hong Kong, linked to San Francisco by the steamships of the White Star Line. I enter Guatemala via the Guatemala City airport, La Aurora, which means "dawn" in Spanish. I first traveled through this place in my mother's womb, headed to Los Angeles on a Pan American Airways flight, no passport or visa required. Later I returned on family visits, first as a kindergartner, and then as an adolescent and as a teenager, going back to see my grandparents and aunts and uncles and cousins; and finally, decades later, as a journalist writing about Guatemala for an American newspaper.

Every time I've traveled to Guatemala I've carried the same hope; that I might discover a bit more about who I am, and unlock the mysteries of my family history. When I was a boy, this was an entirely joyful process consisting of weeks of play with cousins I barely knew and hours sitting at the kitchen tables and in living rooms with my grandparents. As an adult, it's a bittersweet reencounter with the realities of my family's divided existence.

My plane taxis toward the terminal. From my window seat I see lights on the edge of the tarmac, and the old and familiar hangars on the edge of the runway. When I was five or six my mother dressed me up in spiffy suits and leather shoes for this trip; she'd left Guatemala after a shotgun wedding, and she wanted to show the people back home how well she was doing. Once, I arrived in Guatemala wearing the plastic Pan Am wings a flight attendant had pinned on me during the flight. As an adolescent I flew from this airport in an old DC-3 to the jungle, to take in the splendor of the Mayan city of Tikal. And as a college student I visited during the bloody years of civil war and revolution, when right-wing death squads filled the country with terror; I saw air force jets on the taxiways, returning from missions to bomb Mayan villages.

I follow the flow of passengers into the terminal building. During my last visit to Guatemala, in 2007, I witnessed the spectacle of crowds of adoptees with their adoptive parents filling this space, including a cinnamon-skinned girl of about eight with beautiful and striking Indigenous features; she was returning to the country of her birth, and spoke to her adoptive parents in fluent, joyful German. Having heard stories of the baby brokers and the large amounts of money exchanging hands in these adoptions, I felt shame at the thought that my country was selling off its children. Now it's late at night and there are no crowds. I pass through immigration and customs quickly, push open the last doors, and take in the sight of expectant Guatemalan faces, waiting for family reunions to take place.

I see my aunt and uncle. And my mother, a tiny, powerful woman with fair skin and a wonderful, troublemaker's sense of humor. A woman who has never denied me anything I've asked of her, and who often makes me feel inadequate. She raised me when she was in her twenties and it can be said we grew up together, in Los Angeles; like a brother and sister, we fought. I was the unwilling witness to her two divorces and the suicide of her third husband, a norteamericano. Now we embrace and walk toward the terminal door. All is forgiven. When we step outside, I spot a strange sight: two stray dogs, their fur mottled and muttbrown, strutting past the entrance to the parking garage across the street. Most countries put on their best face at the national airport. Qué vergüenza. The dogs sniff and search around the scattered street vendors.

I point out the strays to my aunt, and she tells me there are fewer than there used to be.

TODAY MY MOTHER LIVES IN THE CENTER OF GUATEMALA CITY, in an old property that her great aunt and uncle purchased in the first decades of the last century, the same house where the "street orphan" Ramón grew up. With the last of the money left from her late husband's life insurance policy, my mother hired men to tear down the old adobe walls and to rebuild it with rebar and concrete. She lives here alone, and the pleasant orderliness of the home is offset by the stark solitude I feel. Fresh off the airplane, I have a night of fitful sleep in this home, my slumbers interrupted again and again by cars, trucks, and motorcycles passing on the street outside. I close my eyes and feel as if I've entered the entrails of some old, diesel-fed machine. When I finally drift off to sleep, I have a deeply vivid dream. I'm inside a movie about Guatemala. A death-squad killer is stalking a young Indigenous woman. He shoots an older woman, and suddenly I am the older woman; the bullets pass through me but don't wound me, because in the rules of the dream my body is ghostlike. I follow the younger Indigenous woman as she travels up a river, and now the actor Benicio del Toro is protecting us from the death squads. The dream switches, and I see the stooped back of my late grandfather, standing before a stove, cooking, stirring a large pot. And for a moment I am lifted by the sight of seeing him come back to life.

I wake up to the aroma of the very Guatemalan breakfast my mother is cooking for me. Fried plantains and black beans prepared as frijoles volteados, refried and garnished with a powdery white cheese. People who make frijoles volteados in the United States aren't patient enough to transform them into the light and spongy concoction they become in my mother's Guatemalan hands. "Qué delicia," I tell her. Each bite transports me into the warm, safe domestic spaces of kitchens past. I become a child, a young man, loved, protected, fed the food that has sustained my people for centuries.

NO MATTER WHERE WE FIND OURSELVES, NO MATTER HOW FAR we've traveled, Latino people carry Latin American stories with them. My stories are from Central America; yours may be from Mexico, from South America, or from the Caribbean. The spoken histories passed down to us are threads that serve to bind the divided halves of our family story. The greater the distance in time, the grander and more fantastic the landscapes in these stories become. When I was a very young boy, my mother told me she had grown up poor in Guatemala City, in "a hole in the ground." I imagined her living in an actual hole, an excavated pit with ladders on the side to get out. My mother's metaphor was transformed in my child's mind into the fanciful element of a folktale, a process I can see at work in the stories my students write for me. A father tells his daughter that he walked across open fields in search of a store to buy the alcohol his father craved, and in the daughter's imagination those fields become a vast open plain, a llano "in the middle of nowhere." A mother tells her son that she climbed the mountains near Tijuana to reach the United States, and in the mind's eye of her son those low-slung hills become a range of peaks with Himalayan proportions. The smugglers at the border town become horror-movie monsters; the creeks and streams of the family's ancestral village become wide and turbulent rivers.

Very often, these narratives carry an emotional weight that is difficult for a child-listener to bear. Our guardians tell us that their departure from the home country was an act tinged with regret. "I wanted to give my family the best shot at life," a father says, "even if it meant that I would not be with them." The migrants' decisions to leave, to escape, to tirarse a la aventura, split a family in two, and created a rupture in our personal histories. Our migrant guardians feel compelled to tell us why this happened. Poverty carries many different kinds of humiliation, public and private, and as we listen we can sense the deep shame they once carried. Mijito: My siblings and I were so hungry we fought each other for our food. I was six when my mother left us for her boyfriend. We lived in a cardboard house. Mijita: I never had a birthday party growing up. My mother was always trying to save to buy a plot of land to feed us. We were never recognized by the rest of my father's family, because we were part of his "other" family.

The grim elements in these stories serve as a prologue to a love story of reinvention and resilience, the story of the generation born on U.S. soil, or carried across the border, too young to feel all the hurt the family left behind. The underlying message of these narratives is this: We suffered to give you a life of opportunity in this country. To liberate you from our pain. The message is comforting, in its way: it conveys a sense of parental protection. But the stories themselves (and their repetition, during the entire course of our childhoods) can come to feel like a burden. Once, when I was teaching a class of one hundred undergraduates, and summarizing the history of Latin American immigration, a young man raised his hand and offered this assessment: "The stories our parents tell us—they're just too much. It's like this thing hanging over us. Like nothing we could ever do could be as important as that. As dramatic as that."

MY LATE MATERNAL GRANDPARENTS MARCELO ALVAREZ AND Catalina Villalta are central characters in my family's origin story. My first morning in Guatemala City, my uncle Tono arrives to take me to the neighborhood where Marcelo and Catalina built the only home they ever owned, and where Tono and my aunt Imelda still live. It's called Seis de Octubre, after the date in 1969 when my grandparents and some three hundred other families were granted title to the property. Before we set out, Tono has some news: overnight, a man was shot to death on one of the streets leading into the neighborhood. "We're going to have to take a detour," he says. On the drive, he offers the details of the crime he's heard on the radio: the victim was a twenty-four-year-old driver of a tuk-tuk motorcycle taxi. I've been in the country less than twelve hours and I've been greeted with a murder, as if the killer in my dream had escaped from my subconscious to commit crimes in the real world. A few days later, a group of gunmen will attack the mourners at the funeral of the tuk-tuk driver, and it will be clear that what happened to him was one more event in the cycle of violence fed by Guatemala's small role in the vast, trans-hemispheric business of illegal drugs.

When we finally arrive at la colonia Seis de Octubre, I note the powerful, sweet, rotting smell of trash. My aunt takes me to see my grandparents' old home, which is near the edge of one of the many ravines, or "barrancos," in the middle of Guatemala City. As a boy, I once started a fire in this barranco, by firing bottle rockets into it. When I remind my aunt of this incident, she says grimly: "You wouldn't start a fire there today." The brush is gone, because there is a garbage dump in the barranco now. I walk up to the edge of the ravine, and see what looks like a huge, excavated pit, two hundred feet deep. Several dozen human beings are walking about the floor of the pit, heads bowed over a field of discarded plastic bags, reaching down into the floor of refuse, searching. Vultures circle overhead, drawn by the rotting trash, so many, that my aunt has to wait for them to fly away before she can hang up her laundry. Those vultures are defecating on the neighborhood, and on my beautiful memories of this place. My memories of the Christmas Eves I spent here, when everyone emerged from their homes at midnight, to embrace their neighbors. Of my proud grandfather and wry grandmother and her abundant laughter, and the little, orderly home with the checkerboard tile floor that was their pride and joy.

Did Wong Kim Ark feel this way when he returned to Guangdong? Torn between the familial warmth that surrounded him in his ancestral homeland, and the realities of the poverty and the decadence he saw in the China of the Qing dynasty? In the Guangdong of his day, parents could be forced to sell off a daughter or son to pay off debts. Gangs roamed the countryside and preyed on the poor; floods and crop failures drove people from their land. French and British troops invaded the country, in the name of free markets and the opium trade. Child orphans left to migrate alone across the Pacific to the United States, and he may have seen them on board the ships he took to Hong Kong and back, just as I saw the adoptees crowding the waiting areas at the La Aurora airport.

I see Wong Kim Ark's history and my own and I see parallels between continents and centuries that are seemingly distant from one another. When I enter my aunt and uncle's home in la colonia Seis de Octubre, Tono guides me to a room where he's built a small shrine to Guatemalan history. Its centerpiece is a magazine reproduction of a large painting by Diego Rivera called *Glorious Victory*, the Mexican muralist's commentary on the U.S.-backed coup that overthrew Guatemala's democratically elected government in 1954. The mural shows the architect of that coup, Secretary of State John Foster Dulles, shaking hands with his henchman, the Guatemalan army colonel Carlos Castillo Armas, who became Guatemala's new dictator. They are surrounded by a tableau of victims of an aerial bombing, conducted by CIA-dispatched planes in support of the coup. In the name of anti-Communism and free-market capitalism, the dictators of twentieth-century Guatemala murdered thousands of intellectuals, labor activists, and university students, depositing their bodies on roadsides and in trash dumps in gruesome public displays. The Guatemalan intelligentsia went into exile for two generations. Death squads and military juntas enforced a social order that made us, as a people, less educated and less free-spirited.

"Latino" is a story about empire, and so is "Asian American." The simple fact of continuing to cross back and forth across the Pacific Ocean to keep his family together and prosperous was Wong Kim Ark's own, private act of resistance against the degradations of imperialism. My grandfather was a bricklayer and a union man, and he remained loyal to the cause of working people even through the years of Guatemala's dictatorship. I have a vivid memory of returning to the colonia and hearing my aunt announce that she had caught a glimpse of my grandfather on the television news; she had seen the knotty muscles of his stooped back, and watched him raise his fist and shake it as he stood before a police car that was blocking the advance of a labor-rights march. My grandfather passed the determination to face the degrading power of empire down to his daughter, and she, in turn, raised me with the sense that Guatemala was a land of love and beauty, and that Guatemalan history carried the power to protect me. Wong Kim Ark worked to earn U.S. citizenship for his youngest, Chinese-born son, and that son passed down his own story of immigrant detention (on Angel Island, in San Francisco Bay), to his children, and to his granddaughter, who one day wandered into a federal archive, anxious to research the story of her great-grandfather, Wong Kim Ark.

MY STUDENTS ATTEMPT TO MAKE SENSE OF THEIR SPLIT, MULTI-national family histories in the papers they write for me. They seek to complete a mission they first undertook when they were very young, by asking questions of their guardians and elders. They want to bring their family story into sharper focus, and have a clearer, more grown-up understanding of who they are. One describes a family journey in a Ford truck from California to a town in Michoacán, the vehicle stuffed with luggage and gifts for the long drive; and her arrival in a village of narrow streets, and her encounters with a grandmother she had never met before, and who sits by her front door chewing on pumpkin seeds, watching the town go by, a silent and mysterious figure of womanly strength. Another student laments how her family's long, summer holiday drives to Guerrero are suspended for eight years because an organized crime group has taken over her family's town; when her family can finally return they must sit quietly at her grandmother's home, and avoid wearing "flashy" clothes when she goes out. Others speak of the powerful spiritual forces that loom over their families' ancestral homes. The brujería practiced by certain women in her parents' village is so powerful, one student writes, the men in her family are afraid to go there, because the dark magic of the brujas might cause them to fall in love with one of the village girls. My students walk on cobblestone streets, they hear bells chime for the dead, and they attend wakes; and over the course of their childhoods and young adulthoods their journeys to Latin America teach them how time can transform a place and a country and its people. In this way they learn lessons about history and empire, and these lessons make them feel stronger and more grown-up, and centered.

MY AUNT INTRODUCES ME TO HER NEIGHBORS IN LA COLONIA Seis de Octubre. Benedicto Jimenez, who is eighty-four, tells me how he and my late grandfather and many others built the homes of la colonia, "when this place was nothing but open fields." He tells me of the sons who migrated, including one who is a construction manager in Los Angeles. "My grandson brought me this from California," he tells me, and he produces a stout and silky Stetson hat. Another neighbor, Irma, has six grandchildren in Chicago. And Carlotta, or "Loty," has a daughter and four grandchildren in Harrisburg, Pennsylvania.

On a Valentine's Day sixteen years ago, Loty's daughter Claudia left the colonia with her children to rejoin her husband, who had migrated to the United States. She has never returned. My aunt is the godmother to Claudia's youngest son, which makes them comadres. Claudia is living with her husband and four children in a home they just purchased in Harrisburg: she can't return to Guatemala because she's an undocumented immigrant. "This is what keeps me going," Loty says, and she opens up an album of photographs Claudia has sent from Pennsylvania: Loty's grandson with his father, watching an autumn sunset over the wide Susquehanna River; church pictures; a high school graduation. Loty's family has assimilated into American life. But Loty cannot travel to the United States to see them. She has not seen her family in sixteen years, she tells me, and I think of all the events in my own family in that time span (the birth of a daughter, one college and two high school graduations), and what it would be like to have missed them all.

Loty is in her seventies but when she speaks of her separation from Claudia she seems older. She seems to be shrinking before my eyes, the life-pulse in her squeezed out by the enormous weight of her loss. In this house, she helps care for another daughter's children, and I think of how powerfully intimate this space is. Her daughter Claudia lived and raised children here. In other homes I visit in the Seis de Octubre, I see great-grandparents sharing the space of a home with their great-grandchildren, and a woman in her fifties caring for her octogenarian father. Most Guatemalans grow up with this intergenerational closeness; it's the source of the patience and the perseverance for which guatemaltecos are famous, and for which Guatemalan women are prized as nannies by their U.S. employees. But the familial bonds in Loty's family have been broken. Her family is separated by sixteen years, thousands of miles, and an increasingly impermeable U.S. border. This disconnectedness, repeated a million times over, is the deep, unhealed wound of the Guatemalan present: a people who value family above all else, find themselves deprived of its intimacy.

WONG YOOK JIM TOLD A SAN FRANCISCO JOURNALIST THAT in the course of his life he had spent less than three years with his father, Wong Kim Ark. When his father returned to China to retire, Wong Yook Jim stayed in the United States to work, and the two men were separated again. During World War II, Yook Jim joined the U.S. Marines, but his letters to his father in China stopped going through (much of the country was occupied by the Japanese). Shortly after the war ended, village elders wrote to Yook Jim to tell him his father had died.

The Latino immigrant experience is filled with stories of separation and distant loss. One of my students describes the feelings of her mother upon learning of the death of her parents in Mexico, some twenty years after the mother migrated to the United States as an undocumented immigrant. Crossing the border to see them when they were living would have meant the risk of being separated from her children and the rest of her U.S. family. Now she sees their funerals in photographs, learns the details of the wake in phone calls. The mother laments the "the loss of time she'll never get back with them, the loss of moments she'll never live," my student writes. For two decades in the United States she had worked to send money back to Mexico to help her parents, "and now they're gone and it's as if she has had to reanalyze everything that she's done throughout the last twenty years of her life."

Most Latin American immigrants and their children, documented or undocumented, live with regret, haunted by the life choices that have split their families. My parents migrated just before I was born, and I grew up in the United

States as an only child, separated from my extended family. What kind of person would I have become if I had lived in daily contact with my grandparents, my aunts and uncles and cousins, in a country where I was never treated like an alien or outsider? Our life choices, or the choices of our parents, hang over us. Why did they go down this road, and not the other one? If we erase politics and history and empire from the equation, we can feel like victims of "fate," or our own or our families' ambitions.

BEFORE I SET OUT TO GUATEMALA, I TOLD THE UNIVERSITY class I was teaching that I would be visiting my father's hometown, Gualán, population of forty-five thousand, in the eastern department of Zacapa. Afterward, one of my students approached me to tell me that she, too, has family roots in Gualán. Isabella told me she would ask her mother if my grandfather's name, Francisco Tobar, sounded familiar. Maybe we're related, she said.

As a child and young adult, I listened to my father and uncle Roberto tell me one colorful story after another about life in Gualán; about its old steam train and flowing rivers, and the American-owned banana plantations nearby. Stories about the strange objects on display in the store operated by the United Fruit Company, including baseball bats and gloves for the company's American employees (the sport never caught on in Guatemala). I've long believed that the novelist I later became was born from listening to those stories. When I got older, I heard about the darker side of my father's childhood, the memories of abuse and neglect, and the sense of loss that came from having to end his Guatemalan education at the sixth grade. As I leave Guatemala

City and drive toward Gualán, I know that everything I'm about to see will be colored by the dreamspace of my father's stories, and the sense that I'm entering the terrain of an epic family novel.

I TRAVEL TO GUALÁN WITH MY AUNT FLOR, MY FATHER'S younger half sister. Our car descends from the mountains that cradle the metropolis of Guatemala City into a desert-like landscape, and the asphalt on the highway grows narrower and the lines and markings on the asphalt begin to disappear, until finally we enter a savannah, driving on a plain black strip. We seem to be entering an earlier version of Guatemala, losing decades as we drive farther east. Finally, our car crosses a bridge over the Motagua River, and we enter Gualán. My aunt texts the relative we're going to meet: Carlos Jordán, whose grandmother was my grandfather's sister. He's a second cousin, but we've never met. Carlos texts back with news: he's been contacted by his niece, who told him about my pending arrival. His niece is the mother of my student Isabella. So my student and I are, in fact, related: We're second cousins, twice removed. Small world.

We meet Carlos at his home, which sits on a road in a small valley, surrounded by cornfields and corrals for cattle. Carlos is a retired schoolteacher in his sixties, and soon we're joined by one of his first cousins, Janina, who is a tall and elegant woman with long, white hair. They remember my grandfather well; to them, he was "el tío Pancho." He ran an electric-powered mill for grinding corn at the back of his home, and at lunchtime he'd walk a few blocks and take a midday bath in a watering hole in the Motagua River they called "el pozo de Don Pancho." They tell me more stories about the town. Janina's father used to put her on a donkey for the ride into town to go to school. Carlos remembers the day in the 1960s when a leftist guerrilla army came down from the Sierra de las Minas mountains and occupied Gualán, led by Marco Antonio Yon Sosa, the son of a Chinese immigrant.

Yon Sosa was born in the eastern Guatemalan town of Los Amates, twenty-three miles up the road and rail line from Gualán. He grew up to become an officer in the Guatemalan army; after the coup in 1954, he helped form a leftist guerrilla army, the Movimiento Revolucionario 13 de Noviembre, and became its commander, ambushing army patrols, occupying towns, and blowing up bridges across eastern Guatemala. My cousin Carlos, then a boy of about ten, watched as the mayor pleaded with the Chinese Guatemalan guerrilla commander not to blow up the railroad bridge linking Gualán to the outside word; the rebel forces occupied the town for a few hours, but left the bridge intact.

Like Wong Kim Ark, Yon Sosa's father was from Guangdong. He immigrated from China with his brother in 1912, and they would earn a living in Los Amates selling clothing and shoes, according to research by the Guatemalan historian Arturo Taracena Arriola. Deep in their history, both Gualán and Los Amates resembled the unnamed town and the river that Gabriel García Márquez describes in his novel *Love in the Time of Cholera*. In Gualán, there was a pier on the Motagua River in the center of town, because the Motagua was once navigable and linked Gualán to the Caribbean. Families from elsewhere in Guatemala migrated here (including my grandmother, who was born in the Mayan western part of the country), and from Asia and Europe too. Gualán is still famous for its "beautiful women," Janina tells me, which, I think, is a coded way of saying fair-skinned. There have been songs written to Gualán, she adds, and soon she's sending her daughter to her nearby home to retrieve some lyrics, so she can sing one for me. "¡Qué bonita es mi tierra, qué bonita!" the song begins. The warm light of Gualán hypnotizes those who see it, the song says, and in the end it declares that Gualán is a mirror reflecting "the beauty of Eden."

Janina sings this song as we join a half dozen of my relatives on the porch of a home built by her ancestors early in the twentieth century. There's a hammock nearby, and I can see golden afternoon light on a nearby hillside pasture. I'm invited inside for coffee and cake, and I join my newly discovered relatives in sitting around a dining-room table. Someone turns on a bare bulb whose light feels weak against the purple glow of dusk I can see through the open windows. Night sounds of insects and birds swell around us, and suddenly the verdant, tropical world outside feels huge and borderless. The gray light of the bulb transports me into memories of other Guatemalan nights; my grandparents' kitchen at dinnertime in the Sixth of October, my grandfather slurping his soup, a bare lightbulb glowing above us; a night when I was a boy visiting Gualán and I was very ill, the burning filament of a bulb like this one hovering over me.

I realize now that the light of these Guatemalan memories has never left me. The light of Guatemalan dusk, of its incandescent bulbs. A bit of this village, a place I really knew very little about, was always with me during the long, solitary years of my boyhood in Los Angeles, where I grew up as the only child of a divorced and distracted immigrant woman in her twenties. The Eden glow of Guatemala has stayed with me, decade after decade; I've never stopped feeling its warmth, and I never stopped believing that my family began in a place where rivers flowed and steam trains ran on steel rails. The Guatemalan light in my memory made me stronger and gave me a sense of my place in the world.

OUR LAST STOPS IN GUALÁN ARE THE VACANT LOT WHERE MY grandfather's home once stood and the cemetery where he is buried. I stand before the vacant lot and remember my father's stories about growing up at this spot: the most painful one is about the day his mother and father split, when he was five or six years old. He remembers his mother wrapping up her dishes in paper, preparing to escape with my father's older brother. She could only afford to take one of her two children, and was forced to leave my father alone with his father and his stepmother. "My world was ending. I wanted to disappear." I see the remains of some concrete stairs, weeds growing in the storage room where my father slept, alone, and where he was whipped by his stepmother when he wet his bed or failed to do his chores. Each time I hear him recount these memories, the cloud enveloping him seems to grow thicker. Once, after one of his grandchildren's birthday parties, he turned to my wife and said: "I never had a birthday party when I was growing up." If I conducted an archeological dig here, would I find some rusty, soiled artifact that explained the mystery of his lifelong struggle with feeling unseen and unloved?

We proceed to the cemetery. Flor and I enter a silent metropolis of grave markers, including one with a three-story Chinese pagoda; I can see that the guerrilla leader

Marco Antonio Yon Sosa's family was part of a larger Chinese community in northeast Guatemala. (Many of Yon Sosa's relatives are buried in the cemetery in the town of Huité, about thirty miles from here.) I see quite a few markers with the name Tobar on them, but my aunt walks quickly past them. She's looking for her father, my grandfather, and when she finds the large stone block that contains his remains (and that of three other relatives), I discover there is no marker with his name on it. My grandfather is traveling into eternity anonymously, but he's resting on a peaceful spot, at the top of a hill, with a view of the pretty pasture across the road.

BEFORE I RETURN TO CALIFORNIA, I ASK MY MOTHER TO GUIDE me to one last stop. I want her to show me the neighborhood in Guatemala City where she met my father.

She brings me to a quiet stretch of Sixth Avenue in Zone One of Guatemala City. Only the façade of the building where she lived is still standing: I look through the frame of the shuttered window and I can see blue sky shining through, and I think: the gods of history kept this wall standing just long enough for me to see it. The next earthquake will topple it. My father lived across the street, in the home for street children where his mother worked as a cook—it's now a parking garage. In 1962, the squeal and metallic thump of a car accident at the nearby corner of Sixth Avenue and Twentieth Street brought my future parents out of their homes at the same time. A car had struck a pedestrian and my mother and father joined the crowd of onlookers transfixed, momentarily, by this grim scene. And then my future parents caught each other's eye. In the conversation that followed, in front of a damaged automobile and a dying man, their courtship began. They married after my mother, then nineteen, discovered she was pregnant.

For much of my adult life, the idea that I came to this world as a result of a series of "accidents" hung over me. Doomed to feel like an outsider in both Los Angeles and Guatemala. But seeing this spot for the first time, after a journey that's brought me closer to my family history, I see how silly I've been to think this way.

We live in an age of migrations. When my mother lived here, she was the daughter of a man who had migrated to Guatemala City from a town in its Mayan interior, back in the days when people traveled the fifty or one hundred miles to the capital on foot, sleeping in village plazas along the way. My father was a runaway from Gualán, having escaped from his abusive stepmother, and was living with my grandmother, herself a migrant from the town of Huehuetenango, where her parents had died in an early twentieth-century epidemic. The whole world is on the move and has been for generations. Go to Koreatown or Little Armenia in Los Angeles, or to a Chinese suburb in the Bay Area, or to a Dominican barrio in New Jersey, and you'll find stories of movement and trauma. Over the years, I've found migration stories on Kansas country highways, Pennsylvania battlefields. On this trip, I've learned that Gualán, that small town in a small country where my father was born, is a crossroads too; migrant paths from Guatemala's Indian highlands, Spain, and China meet there.

I am the son of immigrants. To be Guatemalan, to be Latin American, to be Latino or Latinx is to grapple with the promise, the beauty, and the dysfunction of an immigrant life. There is no shame in this, there is nothing wrong with me, I am not broken. My mother became a mother at age twenty and I should forgive the mistakes of her youth. A friend told me many years ago that one day the anger I felt toward my mother would be replaced by compassion; standing on Sexta Avenida and Calle Veinte, at the spot where my private universe came into being, that prophecy has finally come true. If I could, I'd liberate every man and woman in detention at the border, and grant citizenship to every Dreamer, so that they too could see these truths. So they could see what Wong Kim Ark saw when he returned to Guangdong at the end of each of his ocean journeys. I'd show them the epic of their lives, the scenes of their family tragedies and triumphs, the places where desire and hope gave birth to them, and shaped who they are and who they will become.

IN THE FINAL HOURS BEFORE I LEAVE GUATEMALA I DO SOME shopping with my mother, aunt Imelda, and uncle Tono on a sunny afternoon. It's a holiday Monday, and there's a lightness to the city, an unhurriedness. I see so many young couples on motorcycles that I finally quip to my relatives: "When you buy a motorcycle in Guatemala City, is the girlfriend included with it?" The sellers at the city market are cheerful when we haggle with them, and there are parents and children everywhere.

Afterward, I climb to the roof of my mother's house, and take in the view of the neighborhood around us in the final hour before sunset. The noise pollution doesn't bother me anymore. My mother joins me. "So, how do you see Guatemala?" she asks.

"Full of life," I say.

Guatemala is a young country. Youthful energy and familial love are its primary natural resources, more powerful in the global marketplace than all of its coffee, cotton, and bananas put together. The drive of its people is a tidal force, constant, relentless, wearing down obstacles. It's the force that created the Sixth of October neighborhood, and that keeps the garbage collectors working below it. It endured during the years of dictatorship, has survived the bloody years of gang warfare, and lives on in the Age of the Wall, where you can find it at California universities and in the Pennsylvania town where my aunt's comadre lives with her four Guatemalan-born children.

Before I leave, my aunt Imelda takes a moment to make a small farewell speech. All my chapín relatives are great at speeches.

We've been separated by many years, she says. But when she sees me, she feels I am a part of her. Her love for me, and my children, is eternal, she tells me. This is the same speech my students have heard; in person, in the homes of their Mexican and Caribbean and Central American relatives, and over the digital connections of our age, on small screens attached to phone networks. "You are my blood," she says, and her words stay with me in the hours and days after my plane lifts off from the airport whose name means dawn in Spanish.

11

HOME

In his first book, James Baldwin imagined the biological father he never knew. *Go Tell It on the Mountain* is an autobiographical novel that tells the story of "John," an African American adolescent growing up, like Baldwin did, in Harlem. "Richard" is the name Baldwin gives to John's father, and when he enters the story we find him reading a book. Richard moves from rural Maryland to New York City with John's fictional mother-to-be, Elizabeth, and as their love affair progresses, he takes her on dates to the American Museum of Natural History and the Metropolitan Museum of Art. Often, they are the only Black people in those places, because they are living in a time, the 1920s, when African Americans are the lowly outcasts of New York City society, its cleaning women and its laborers. Against this, Richard asserts his humanity by soaking in as much of the culture and civilization of New York as he can. He takes Elizabeth to see plays, shows her the Met's paintings and its African masks, and is determined, Baldwin writes, "to get to know everything them white bastards knew." This is the father Baldwin wanted to have, the home he wanted to live in: a family with a proud Black man at its center, a man who would show his family the grandeur and beauty of human creation, and all its possibilities.

Several decades later, and in real life, you could find my mother and father and me in the museums of Los Angeles, California. The longing of people of color, and of the people of the "Global South," of immigrants and outcasts to be connected to the world of civilization and culture is a universal one. I remember, most vividly, the Los Angeles County Museum of Art, with its multistory, indoor atrium, and all the wonders contained there. The caskets of three-thousand-year-old Egyptian mummies, Greek sculptures, and paintings of foggy English seaports and bright impressionist landscapes from the South of France, and Aztec and Mayan and Incan jade and gold. That museum was the story of the world, and my parents wanted to present me with all its mystery and splendor. And my father, especially, wanted to soak it all in himself. He had been born in a village in Guatemala, a place frozen in time, and now he was in an American metropolis where the boundaries of time did not exist, and you could peer into humanity's past, and see into its future. To be in the presence of all those objects of beauty and art made him feel alive and complete.

My father took portraits of me with books. In a home he filled with books. The deeply engrained reading habit my mother and father encouraged in me brought me, a few decades later, to the work of James Baldwin, the author who is, in many ways, the literary father of this work. As a boy, Baldwin stood before the lions at the New York Public Library and entered its maze of books; I stepped inside the Hollywood branch of the Los Angeles Public Library and received my first library card, a rectangle of white paper that allowed me to take home any one or half dozen of the volumes in its collection. I would bring those books home and place them in the small bookcase my parents bought for me. In this way I brought my family's story to its apotheosis. This is the migrants' dream: to see their families assert their humanity in this new country built on ideas of freedom and justice. To show we are thinking people and not just brawn and sweat. And more than that, to revel in and enjoy our time on this Earth, freed at last of ancient and degrading oppressions, and of the legacy of conquests past. Latinx immigrant families dream of building homes filled with small, beautiful objects (a painting of Don Quixote on the wall, or a print of a Diego Rivera), of sharing good food with family and friends on a weekend afternoon. At these moments of relaxation and repose, they think: this is the Eden we crossed deserts and oceans to reach. A home with a place to paint, or a big, comfortable chair to sit in and read under a lamp, with a cushion under the small of our backs: these are not small things to people with memories of dirt floors and concrete walls in their pasts.

An interviewer once asked me when I was happiest: "When I see my children reading" was my answer. I feel deep emotion when I hear my sons and daughter engage in witty wordplay, or when I hear them discuss matters of history and art, because I can remember the Latin American poverty and illiteracy in my family's near past, and because I have seen my own family members humbled and humiliated by the micro- and macro-aggressions of racism in the present. When my wife and I purchased the home in which we raised our children, she designed an eight-foot-tall series of shelves to occupy the largest wall in our living room, and over the years we filled it with picture books and children's dictionaries, and Shakespeare plays and art history books, and cookbooks to teach us the nuances of Mexican cuisine.

This longing to embrace sensuous, intellectual, and aesthetically pleasing pleasures is older than James Baldwin, older than the United States, older than even the idea of "race." The Greek thinker Epicurus described such a way of living in the fourth century before Christ; his philosophy was popularized in the first century BCE by the Roman poet Lucretius. To be human is to seek peace and freedom from fear, Epicurus taught. Human society was born in a primitive battle for survival, and our highest goal should be the pursuit of happiness and the absence of suffering. The exercise of reason is the key that opens the door of a life well lived. From these ideas, the word "epicurean" was coined. Over the years, I've met many epicurean immigrants and Latinxes; I've placed them in my novels, or simply enjoyed their company. They are readers and lovers of good food, poets in their free time, writers of love letters and personal manifestos, collectors of objects of affordable beauty. They are dancers, farmworkers, artists, store clerks, amateur historians. I've visited their homes and heard them describe their families' struggles to build a home free of hurt and want. I've seen them create a version of themselves that is more alert and wiser and worldly, even as the rest of the United States ignores them, or treats them as a caste of lesser humans, the hired help of America. Even as they remain invisible in American mass media, they are everywhere. I've found them in all the corners of the United States I've visited.

AS A KID, I WAS A MAP GEEK. I DREW MAPS OF MY NEIGHBOR-hood and of the Southern California freeway system, and I collected gas-station road maps. Now, as a grown-up, I set off from Los Angeles three times, seeking to make progress across the pages of my *National Geographic Road Atlas*. My mission is to hit the highway and see the United States of America. Eventually, I will log about seventeen thousand miles on these trips. I drive from California to Oregon, a state where I worked for a few years, teaching students who were "white," and meeting many white people who were not especially privileged. Here, I once conversed with a home-less taxi driver who slept in his car, and at the University of Oregon I listened to my students tell me stories about the dysfunction and malaise in their white families and com-munities. Now, in early December, I drive through Oregon's evergreen and misty landscape, past its forests of Douglas fir trees, to the plains of the Willamette Valley, and one of its Latino farmworker towns, Woodburn.

I meet with Teresa Alonso León, who was born into a Purépecha Indigenous family from the Mexican state of Guerrero. She tells me of her childhood in Oregon, and the hard winters her family suffered after they migrated and established a home there, and the racism they frequently encountered. Teresa is round-faced, in her forties, not tall in stature, and proud and centered and driven. We talk about her journey to the United States as a young girl, and how she was separated from her mother, and the story veers to the time she and an aunt were detained at the border and she was placed, briefly, in an orphanage in Tijuana. For much of her childhood in Oregon she lived with the pos-sibility of being deported. "That was everybody's constant fear. We didn't talk about it in my house, but I knew about it. I heard adults talking about it." There were three languages spoken in her orbit, but young Teresa was the first true master of the one that was spoken outside her home: English. On excursions into white Oregon, she translated for her parents, omitting the insults she heard. "It was constant, throughout my life, I chose what to translate back to my parents. Because there was so much racism." Now she is a U.S. citizen and was elected by the residents of Woodburn, Gervais, and other farm towns to a seat in the Oregon state legislature.

Listening to Alonso León tell me the story of Woodburn and its constellation of farm towns, I see how a Mexican history, a Latino history, and an Indigenous history are embedded in the landscape around me. I wander through Woodburn's brick-and-mortar downtown, past its Mexican restaurants and a clothing store stocked with boots and Stetsons and huipiles and embroidered Mexican dresses. A half century ago these storefronts housed other businesses that catered to white people, while bracero laborers lived on the town's fringes, unaware that one day Spanish would become one of the town's primary languages, and that Mexican people would one day build permanent homes here. In the 1970s, immigration agents raided the surrounding fields, running over berries and cauliflower, and yet Woodburn and Gervais are still mestizo towns. Before Alonso León was an American, she was Mexican, and before that she was Purépecha, but when we speak she is organizing a conference of "Latino" elected officials. Latino is an alliance, a convergence of common interests. Home in Oregon is an island of Latinidad surrounded by threat and prejudice, where once a year Alonso León and her family perform Purépecha dances at the town's annual Fiesta Mexicana parade.

After we part, I return to non-Latino Oregon, with its unhoused "travelers," and other unrich people who are proud and adrift, and who have no story or theory to explain their hardships. And it strikes me how "Latino" is a shield of unity that protects our people, and that gives them a sense of common purpose, in this unraveling country we call home.

THE ROAD TAKES ME INTO THE WOODS OF CENTRAL OREGON, past the ashy ruins of dozens of homes destroyed in recent wildfires, and then across the scrublands of the eastern Oregon desert, and into decaying, one-stoplight towns with billboards offering help to the agnostic and the suicidal. I can feel the suffering of white people embedded in this landscape, but this suffering has no socially acceptable name, no slogan embraced by the mass media. There is no "Black Lives Matter" here or "Sí se puede." And then, in Nyssa, Oregon, I see a large sign, painted above a water tank: COWBOY LIVES MATTER. I reach Wilder, in western Idaho. The same circuit of itinerant work that brought Alonso León's family to the Pacific Northwest brought Mexican families here.

My drive through the December landscape of fallow fields brings me into the town's handful of square blocks. I introduce myself to the first and only person I see walking the frigid streets. He's a twentysomething son of farmworkers who isn't a U.S. citizen but who is a Donald Trump supporter, because he believes Joe Biden is going to raise everyone's taxes. Over at his job at a local auto-parts store, all of his white coworkers are worried about this, and he's internalized their libertarian unease about the growth of government. He can't vote, he tells me, but if he could, he would have voted for Trump. I'm not as surprised by this as you might think: to have a Mexican-born immigrant express his support for a man who has insulted and demeaned Mexican immigrants. Like anyone else, he wants to fit in. When you are surrounded by so much conservativism a little bit of it can't help but stick to you, small flakes of Republican confetti, each glimmering like tiny bits of gold and paper money. "I would admit he's racist, he talks a lot of smack. I don't think he's fit for office," he tells me. "But the way the country is, you never want a lot of money out of your paycheck. I guess everyone is looking out for themselves." American individualism is a powerful thing. The idea that you can fill your wallet with honestly earned U.S. dollars, your own piece of the American dream. It can even persuade a Mexican immigrant from Manzanillo, Colima, to support a man who is bent on deporting as many other Mexican immigrants as he can.

We say goodbye and my interviewee enters a large trailer home that's been affixed to a patch of Wilder real estate, dormant rose bushes in the front yard. Latino identity, like that of other American ethnic groups, is a series of paradoxes created by the attraction and repulsion to white Anglo-Saxon Protestant values. We see WASP life as this orderly, safe, and affluent state of being, and many of us seek to live inside it. We want to build our homes inside the neat, uncluttered space we imagine "white" people to inhabit; even as a darker, unseen, unspoken tradition of prejudice, conflict, and violence surrounds those spaces in real life. Beyond the dormant hop fields I can see on the edge of town, white farmers once brought old railroad cars for their Mexican workers to live in, and people slept there in these cold and dusty spaces like so much baggage; and the Oregon Trail once ran nearby, and the Shoshone were dispossessed; and there is the road upon which American citizens of Japanese descent were shipped from Seattle and Portland and other cities of the Pacific Northwest to an internment camp on the Idaho steppes.

ON MY DRIVE TO UTAH THE WINTER LANDSCAPE IS A DOZEN different shades of brown. The burnt umber of a newly plowed field; the brown mustard of dormant grasses. I cross the old frontier between Mexico and the United States, the forty-second parallel. When I reach Salt Lake City, and head for its westside, the faces in the cars around me are brown. West of the railroad tracks is home to the city's Latino barrio. I decide that Salt Lake City feels a little like L.A. to me; only with drier air and taller mountains and less traffic.

I arrive at the home of Andrew Alba, who described himself on the phone to me as "this brown kid covered in drywall dust all day." For years, he's paid the bills working in construction. Oil painting is his passion, however. Alba directs me to his studio he's built in an old carport next to his home, which itself is adjacent to an old westside creek that's been cemented over into a drainage ditch. He is in his midthirties, and after many years of effort, galleries have begun to exhibit his work; in 2020 he earned an arts fellowship from the state of Utah. Lately, he's been placing more brown-skinned figures at the center of his canvases. The other day, a local artist and friend commented: "So, you're a political artist now." And this made Alba laugh, because, as he told me, he's just painting brown people.

Andrew Alba's father is the Mexican American son of farmworkers who stopped their wanderings on the migrant trail two generations ago. His mother is white, and he grew up Mormon in an overwhelmingly white neighborhood of Salt Lake called Sugar House. He was one of six children; as in many mestizo families, the Alba siblings range widely in color, from those who could pass for white, to those, like him, who could not. "I love my skin color," he tells me. "It's a type of raw sienna." In junior high, his classmates called him "dirt skin" and he learned that many of his fellow Mormons believed dark complexion was "the curse of Cain." It bothered Alba that the church wouldn't allow Blacks into the priesthood, and he stopped being Mormon at age sixteen. Becoming an artist was an assertion of his humanity in the face of the racialism around him. In a very literal sense, he's painting over the idea that his "dirt skin" makes him an inferior human being. Alba and his wife, who is white, moved to the west side of Salt Lake so that their kids could be around more people of color, so that they could see the idea of home in this community of brown people, of Spanish-speakers and Chicanos, of old pickup trucks and taquerías.

Later, Alba will direct me to the Salt Lake City site where a Latino man was killed by police; in the year of George Floyd, this spot has been transformed into a series of murals that memorialize many different people of color killed by police. A powerful identification with the struggles of other Latinx peoples is as much an element of our collective identity, I think, as the individualism I saw in Idaho. After the 2019 mass shooting targeting Mexican Americans and Mexican people at a Walmart in El Paso, Andrew had a weeping cowboy and the city's name tattooed on his forearm.

"Have you ever been to El Paso?" I ask.

"No," he says.

AS IT HAPPENS, I AM HEADED TO EL PASO. BUT FIRST I CROSS through Colorado and reach New Mexico, tracing the footsteps of the conquerors who pushed the frontiers of New Spain to territories still inhabited by many different nations of Pueblo Indians; in the landscape of piñon forests and rocky canyons and buttes I feel transported back to those distant centuries. Finally, I arrive in the semi–ghost town of Tierra Amarilla, with its tumbling storefront ruins. This is the site of a 1967 uprising against Anglo encroachment on the land grants made to the Spanish settlers, led by the charismatic preacher Reies Lopez Tijerina. The movement climaxed with an armed raid on the Tierra Amarilla courthouse. I find a faded tribute to the "T.A. Raiders" painted on the wall of an abandoned storefront—but no people. Finally, on the outskirts of the town, I see the occasional truck pulling up to Henry's, a liquor and hardware and fishing supply store. The clerk inside is named C. J. DeYapp, and he is the twenty-six-year-old grandson of the store's late founder, Henry Ulibarri, a man who knew Lopez Tijerina back in the day. Ulibarri, I learn later, is a surname with Basque origins, and the name of a Spanish settler/conqueror who passed through these parts in the first decade of the eighteenth century. "As far as my nana's side," C. J. tells me, "they for generations have been in Cebolla," a town twelve miles to the south. "My tío Rick is the local electrician," he adds, and his tías live and work in the surrounding settlements; one does nails in Santa Fe. It's a Sunday and most of C. J.'s customers are buying beers and liquor shooters to take home for family gatherings; he seems to know them all on a first-name basis. Standing before his cash register,

I feel as if I've entered Tierra Amarilla's community living room.

When I pass through Cebolla, I see a ranch with a sign declaring ULIBARRI. The Spanish explorer Juan de Ulibarrí carved his name on the cliffs of northern New Mexico in 1701 and 1709, in expeditions against the Navajo, and I marvel at the fact that a place of such natural beauty and peacefulness can contain so much history of ethnic conflict. Violence made this a "Hispanic" place, and Hispanic remains the preferred nomenclature for people with names like Ulibarrí and Archuleta. I travel on, southward, to the affluence of Santa Fe, a town where the Native people once rose up and slaughtered the Spaniards, and where the new name for ethnic conflict and displacement is "gentrification." I follow a highway that runs parallel to the narrow canyon of the Rio Grande, and soon I am in Albuquerque, and the land flattens out, and I am on an empty desert plain.

ONE OF THE PLEASURES OF BUILDING A HOME IS TO FILL IT with the small things a home needs. Cutlery, cookware, rugs, flowerpots. Sweaters for your children. A clock for their bedrooms. Storage boxes. Lawn sprinklers. Groceries. In El Paso, you can buy all those things at the Gateway West Walmart. Twenty-three people were killed there, while shopping for the objects to fill their private, domestic universe. Their murderer was a gunman who targeted brown-skinned people in an act of self-described ethnic warfare. Now, sixteen months later, I stand in the parking lot and I see a steady stream of shoppers filing through the same entrance he used. I'm stunned to find the place open, and to see people walking about the massive store as if nothing had happened. Just past the glass doors where a security camera captured the gunman walking into the store with a WASR-10 semiautomatic rifle, I find racks of women's polyester parkas and boxes of donuts for sale. The light is fluorescent, stark, and not of this world.

In an online manifesto, the shooter said he wanted to make Texas a white state. He feared the power of Latino voters, and the "great replacement" of white people from Texas. And now it feels as if official, corporate El Paso has tried to erase the Latino, Mexican, and Mexican American dead. Why else would you allow acts of cold, callous commerce to continue on the site of such a horror? All there is to mark the crime that unfolded here is a new memorial in the parking lot. Monuments to mass carnage often render the dead as geometric abstractions, and here they are represented by twenty-two aluminum tubes joined together into a tower; at the site of the McDonald's in San Ysidro, California, where twenty-one people were killed, there is a sculpture made of twenty-one marble hexagons; at Virginia Tech, there are thirty-two limestone squares. Unable to come to grips with the racist roots of the murderous act that unfolded here, or to make a statement about United States history, white supremacy, gun violence, and Mexican and Tejano culture, El Paso's civic leaders have erected a nondescript work of public art; it fades into the asphalt landscape of the parking lot that surrounds it, in the same way a cell-phone tower or an electrical transformer might. I park next to it, one hundred yards from the entrance, and watch shoppers come and go without visiting or looking at it. The memorial does not unsettle the people who enter its orbit, or even draw their attention. The social and business order of the United

States is built on looking away from and forgetting the violence that created it, and the hatreds that sustain it. When I walk deeper into the Walmart itself, I see masked shoppers (there is a sudden resurgence of the pandemic here), and I hear the steady beeping of their purchases at the registers of the self-serve checkout.

ON THE OTHER END OF EL PASO, THERE IS A COMMUNITY AND A ghost town called Duranguito. I meet Antonia Morales there. She is one of the last two remaining holdouts to a city redevelopment project that would expel her from her longtime home to build a new arena. In recent years, Antonia has stood firm and refused to leave, bulldozers and eviction notices be damned. She is ninety-two years old, and white-haired, spry, and salty of speech. And, like many people in El Paso, she is a true child of fronterizo culture. She was born in nearby Columbus, New Mexico, twelve years after that border town was raided by Pancho Villa, and then moved to Ciudad Juárez, and finally to El Paso. Duranguito was a tough neighborhood when she arrived in the 1960s, and she found herself chasing out prostitutes. "Lárguense de aquí, cochinas!" she would yell at them, and in this fashion, using a term that means "sluts" in Spanish, she defended her new home. Back then, El Paso and Ciudad Juárez were like a single, midsize town with a river running through the middle, and people crossed the border bridges with ease. Sometimes, the U.S. border agents didn't even bother to check your papers, she tells me. "They would just say, 'Hi, how are you?'"

Crossing the border today is an ordeal of lines and scanners and fences and electronic scanners and dogs with vigilant noses. But you can still climb the hills of El Paso and see the panorama of Juárez on the other side, and take in the binational metropolis as a single entity, a light-brown patina of desert dust coloring its air and its streets, and the concrete river channel and the fences that run through its center.

NEXT, I DRIVE FOR TWO DAYS THROUGH ONE OF THE EMPTY quarters of Texas, past longitude after longitude of brushland and dry riverbeds, a region without cattle, or even roadkill. The border is to the right of my car, and sometimes I can glimpse it, or sense it in the landscape; a green canyon with the brown stripe of the Rio Grande running through it. I reach the Rio Grande Valley and the river that is the U.S. border comes into focus; a barrier so narrow, I could easily toss a stone across it. In the town of Rio Grande City I talk to a Mexican American Trump supporter—she's easy to find, there's a big Trump flag in her front yard. María professes a deep disdain for the country of her ancestors, which is about four hundred yards to the south. "The only good thing there are the avocados," she says. "And I don't like chile or cilantro either." I chuckle at the exuberance of her intolerance, and she laughs with me. María is a large woman in her fifties, a schoolteacher, and she tells me that her support for Trump has made her an object of scorn at her workplace ("They call me Mrs. Trump"), and so she doesn't talk politics much when she leaves home. But when she's home she raises her Trump flag and an Old Glory too. The personalities on her large-screen television, which is most often tuned to the same cable-news channel, invite her to fight for her country, the United States of America, against the forces of racial tolerance and economic equality. This, too, is a plank in the improvised architecture of Hispanic identity. The yearning for an order free of abortion rights, welfare, and gay marriage, and other sins foisted upon a pious, Christian people. In these homes, a white Jesus of light-brown locks looks down upon us from a portrait in our living rooms, blood dripping from the crucifixion-wounds in his palms. He smiles upon us, beneficently, and we sense he is pleased with our religious rigor, with the obedience we demand of our children and the extra layer of wax we spray on our furniture.

I ENTER EAST TEXAS AND LOUISIANA, PASSING THROUGH cities and rural counties rich with African American history. In New Orleans I wander briefly through the Ninth Ward, and the semirural cityscape reminds me of the sultry towns of Guatemala's Caribbean coast, where salty sea breezes flow through a landscape of tumbledown wood houses and palm trees. Finally, I reach the urban sprawl of Metro Atlanta, and a ranch-like suburb of curving roads and thin pine trees. A Mexican immigrant named Gustavo recently purchased a home here, his own little piece of New South affluence. He's a construction worker, in his fifties, and when he moved here his mexicano friends warned him this subdivision would be filled with "gente country," i.e., good old boys who hate Mexicans. But his new neighbors have given him a friendly Southern welcome. "I've accomplished a lot, considering the closed doors I had," he tells me in Spanish. In Mexico, Gustavo was unable to pursue his education past high school. His family ran a small store in Mexico City, and he has memories of his daughter, then a toddler, reaching up to a counter for the candies they sold. He brought his family to Georgia twenty years ago, when it was the exotic new frontier of the Latino immigrant experience. He took jobs in construction, despite knowing nothing about the craft. Now he operates a small remodeling business and his daughter, a DACA recipient, is about to graduate from Harvard. He's been undocumented and has not seen his family in Mexico since he left twenty years ago. Gustavo's success is tinged with the stigma of his status, the boldness of his actions; it's as if he's sailed across the seas and burned his ship when he arrived at his destination. He likely will retire as an undocumented person. But this is not what defines him. We stand on the backyard deck of his new home and look out into the small patch of Georgia forest that belongs to him; the sense of personal accomplishment is palpable. He is a fit man of mestizo features who works with his hands but has a deep hunger for intellectual conversation. "I like poetry," he tells me. "Sometimes poems contain a lot of wisdom." He mentions the compositions of the famous singer-songwriters of the Latin American left, like Facundo Cabral and Alberto Cortez, and says he is proud of the fact that he never used corporal punishment against his children. He confesses to me that "I am a person with a temper. Impulsive. Over the years I've learned to control that, to overcome it."

I travel next to the center of Atlanta to visit a "Dreamer." Yehimi Cambrón, twenty-eight, crossed the border as a child, walking through the Arizona desert, and then "stacked like tuna" in a Suburban. These days, she's an artist who has painted several murals across Atlanta celebrating the city's diversity. We meet underneath a six-story mural she painted in the city's Hapeville district. Cambrón is tall, slender, and filled with generational attitude. "In some spaces, I will be white-passing, and there will be privilege in that," she tells me. "Other times: God, I feel undocumented as fuck." Take, for example, the words stamped on the Georgia driver's license she got after her DACA application went through: "Limited Term." That's one more chip on her shoulder, she says, added to so many others. Like the time she was ten and she won an art contest but her teachers said they couldn't give her the fifty-dollar cash prize because she didn't have a Social Security number. Her paintings are celebrations of Latinx fortitude and ethnic diversity, and her Hapeville mural features a Blaxican boy and his African American mother, reaching for butterflies (a symbol of the undocumented) painted on a wall twelve minutes from Martin Luther King Jr.'s Ebenezer Baptist Church. When I leave her, I try to imagine what a King speech about the undocumented and the Black Lives Matter moment would sound like. What Bible passages would the great speaker cite, which rhythmic phrases would he bring to his peroration?

I ENTER FLAT FLORIDA, ON A LIGHTED CORRIDOR OF LONG straightaways that guide me into the foreboding darkness of a moonless night, cutting through the habitat of feral hogs, bobcats, and wild turkeys. Cuban Miami is waiting for me at the end of this drive. I reach Little Havana late the next morning, and I shed my last layer of winter fleece and feel beads of sweat dripping down my temples. The last time I was here, I was reporting on the case of five-year-old Elián González, the Cuban refugee who landed in Florida in 1999 after an ill-fated ocean journey. Now I discover that the block where he lived during the ensuing months-long custody battle has been renamed "Elizabeth Brutons Way" by the city of Miami (with her name misspelled on the sign) in honor of his drowned mother. I find a block where three different Central American families live, natives of El Salvador, Nicaragua, and Guatemala. There's a Peruvian restaurant. And in the small parking lot outside the Va Cuba travel agency I introduce myself to three Cubano seniors. A woman, her husband, and her sister-in-law, all in their seventies, graying and dressed in the frumpy casualwear of the struggling South Florida middle class.

I ask them about the recent election, which has finally been called for Joe Biden. "If this government that's coming to power is socialist, what's coming is very dark," one of the women tells me. "Cuba has suffered sixty years of poverty, tragedy, disaster, shortages . . . Where Communism takes root, not even weeds grow."

The woman is planning a visit to her family in Cuba, and she is afraid the Cuban government will retaliate against them if their names are printed, so I don't ask her name. She hates the dictatorship. And yet . . . "If it hadn't been for Fidel Castro, my children in Cuba wouldn't have studied," she tells me. "They would have been shining shoes and selling newspapers in the street. Because they [the Communists] did one good thing: they taught the people to read and write." Her children and grandchildren became doctors and dentists—who now rely on their American relative's remittances to get by.

"I don't agree with capitalism," the woman's sister-in-law says. She is in her sixties, intelligent, and I sense she has a powerful truth to share with me. "Capitalism is hard," she continues. "You have to work, and sweat, and earn what you eat . . . But wherever they take freedom from you, no system works." In Cuba, she was employed at a university's humanities department, and saw the bright people there cowed into silence. Not long after her son was arrested for making "anti-revolutionary" statements on a city bus, he left Cuba in the mass exodus of the 1980 Mariel boatlift, when the Castro regime allowed thousands to leave the island. The Cuban government repeatedly denied her an exit visa to travel to the United States and live with him, and she didn't see him for twenty years. During those years, the Straits of Florida, the Florida Current, and the Gulf Stream were a chasm at the center of her home, a whirlpool of roiling, deadly waters separating her from her son as he grew into manhood and middle age.

"All that I've suffered," she says. Todo lo que he sufrido.

I tell her that I've just heard a story from a Mexican immigrant who's been separated from his family for twenty years. "To be latinoamericano is to suffer," I say.

"Seguro que sí," she says. Without a doubt.

The Cuban and the Mexican immigrant experiences are portrayed in the United States media as opposites of social class and political outlook. But now I've found this emotional commonality. We people grouped together under the tent named "Latino" are living with the hurt caused by war and politics, conquest and surrender, revolution and dictatorship. We have seen borders redrawn and fortified by the American empire, and by the conflicts set off by its imperial ambitions. We have crossed those borders, by land, air, or sea, in a near or distant past, and the love, the divisions, and the regrets in our families reach across those borders. Our ancestors have escaped marching armies, coups d'état, secret torture rooms, Stalinist surveillance, and the outrages of rural police forces. And now we stand in the United States, on a Miami street corner, or in an Atlanta suburb, working to pull the strands of our family history together, and to make ourselves feel whole, again.

AS I DRIVE THROUGH SNOWY NEW JERSEY, I SEE A SCI-FI apparition on the horizon. Glimmering and mirage-like inside refracted waves of winter sunlight. The towers of Gotham! New York City, at long last. I navigate throughways and past tollbooths and across bridges into upper Manhattan, the old stomping grounds of James Baldwin. I enter Spanish Harlem. I park my car, put on my winter coat, and take to El Barrio's sidewalks; I hear two, three different reggaetón songs. "Dile que tú eres mía, mía / Tú sabe' que eres mía, mía." El Barrio moves to the creations of reggaetoneros even with snow and ice on the ground like there is today. Let's pause for a moment to appreciate the journey of that "Latino" music genre. Born from influences of United States hip-hop and Dominican dembow, with bits of Panama and Colombia and Atlanta trap music thrown in, and forged in the underground scene of San Juan housing projects, reggaetón eventually reached boom boxes in Spanish Harlem and other barrios of the Puerto Rican diaspora, to be commercialized and transmitted to billions of streaming smartphones around the world. I expect to see Bad Bunny strutting down the street at any moment. Instead, I find a friendly older Nuyorican gentleman scraping the snow from the front stairs to his basement brownstone apartment.

Rolando Cortez is a diesel mechanic and a student of El Barrio history, and when I tell him about my cross-country drive and my writing mission, he rattles off the names and places and icons of the Puerto Rican renaissance of the sixties and seventies. We are standing where all those events unfolded, he tells me. And he witnessed many of them, as a young man. The militant revolutionaries named the Young Lords, the artists of Taller Boricua, El Museo del Barrio, and the poetry of Pedro Pietri, a cofounder of the Nuyorican Poets Café. Rolando's erudition and Puerto Rican pride go back to his childhood, he tells me. His mother, despite being "broke" and struggling to make ends meet in her work as a beautician, bought the family a complete set of the *Encyclopedia Britannica* when he was a child; his father was a barber who "knew everybody" and who, late in life, "was a numbers runner." Of himself, Rolando says: "I was a hustler. In the sense that I worked my ass off." He once wanted to be an aeronautical engineer (an unfulfilled dream of my father as well). But he became a young parent and instead worked as a mechanic for various New York utilities, saving up enough from his union jobs to own the big brownstone before us, in a neighborhood on the cusp of gentrification. He invites me to the local bodega and buys us coffee. "Hey, muñeca," he says when a woman friend walks past. We talk for two hours; about the history of racial classifications in Puerto Rico, jíbaro music, the Italians and the Jews he grew up with, and the story of "Todd, the white guy next door."

Cortez tells me his Puerto Rican grandfather had the blue-gray eyes of the Canary Islands, but he lived in a bohío, the traditional thatched-roof hut of the Taino people. His father had high Taino cheekbones and curly hair, "as a result of being mixed." In East Harlem, this kind of Caribbean multiethnicity interacts with New York City cosmopolitanism, producing a quantum physics of cultural diversity. I see a white woman walk past in an elegant parka, and when a mestizo man walks past, Rolando says, "Mexicanos, good people." After we part, I walk down Lexington Avenue and see a locked bicycle whose handlebars are festooned with Guatemalan flags. Later I will study the census data for this tract and find it is 57 percent "Hispanic" and 33 percent "Black." From others I meet in Spanish Harlem I will learn about the symbiosis between Puerto Rican and African American history and politics here, a relationship born in the intimacies shared in the neighborhood's public-housing towers, and in the "mixed blood" of the island itself.

IN DRIVING ACROSS THE UNITED STATES, I FEEL LIKE I AM watching different parts of my family story unfold along the road and at all the stops I make. I see my ambitious father again and again in the strangers I meet—and also my mother's cheeky wit, my angry conservative relatives, and the "raza" undergrads with whom I shared college adventures back in the day. Every Latino person is not a stranger, even if there is something exotic (to my California-born eyes) about all the different places they are living. I am finding a little bit of myself in all the ecologies and time zones of the United States I visit. In a strange way, the trip is making me feel more "American" than ever.

ON THE ROAD WEST, I STOP IN PATERSON, NEW JERSEY, FA-mous for the work of the poet William Carlos Williams, who was of Puerto Rican, English, and French Caribbean heritage. I see Dominican and Puerto Rican flags painted on the side of a bodega. Jahmier, eighteen, and his girlfriend, Ana, seventeen, are inside, working behind the counter. They are a young and handsome couple, enjoying a workday that is also like a date. "My dad is Dominican, and my mom is Puerto Rican," Jahmier says. He doesn't speak Spanish, but Ana does; she's a dominicana born on the island. Ana remembers the way kids in Paterson made fun of her accent when she was in grade school. "After a while, I realized: I know two languages. I'm going places, and you're not." She is a fan of Cardi B, the Bronx-born Dominican Trinidadian hip-hop artist. "I like the way she handles herself. And she represents the Hispanic community, and the Black community. And she also represents women empowering themselves." I describe my cross-country mission to them, speaking with that L.A. accent I can't shake, one that contains notes of Chicanos and cholos and surfers and paisas and assorted California bohemians. When I give Jahmier my business card, he runs his fingers over its letters and the embossed seal of a California university. And suddenly I feel as if I'm an ambassador from some other territory, another, distant republic of Latinidad.

THE HEART OF PENNSYLVANIA IS PHALLIC STEEL SILOS AND rolling farmland. I cross this idyllic landscape and arrive in Harrisburg, home to Claudia, the daughter of Loty, the woman I met a year earlier at the colonia Seis de Octubre in Guatemala City. Claudia and her husband live a few blocks from the Susquehanna River in central Harrisburg, in a home they purchased recently for the astonishingly low price of $35,000. Now in their forties, they've raised their four children in Harrisburg; two of those children have become adults, working at a bank and as a manager at a financial services company. They tell me how a few months after my visit to the colonia in Guatemala, Loty had turned gravely, terminally ill. They witnessed the drama of Loty's final days via their phones, with Claudia torn over whether she should return to Guatemala to see her mother before she died.

"I'm going to come," Claudia told her Guatemalan relatives. "Let me see how I can do it." But then she sat down in her Harrisburg home with her husband and four children, all of whom were grown up enough to have opinions about what she should do. If she traveled to Guatemala, there was a good chance she might not be able to return to Pennsylvania, because she remains undocumented. Her family's final verdict was: "No, we need you here."

On the phone, Claudia spoke with her dying mother one last time. "If you want to come, come then," her mother said, in an embittered voice. "If you don't, don't." It was an awkward and awful way for Claudia to end her relationship with the woman who had brought her into the world. After the funeral, which, it goes without saying, Claudia could not attend, more bitterness followed. Claudia argued, via telephone, with her adult brother over the fate of the family's home in the colonia, where he still lived. She believed getting her brother out of that home would be in his best interest. "I don't care if the whole colonia turns against me."

Each time Claudia clicked off the WhatsApp connection to Guatemala, she returned to her Pennsylvania life. With each passing day, the burning fire of anxiety and anger and regret she felt about the country and the people she left behind tormented her a little less. She and her husband and her four children have built something beautiful in this Harrisburg home of theirs, in this strange country that is now, in so many ways, their country. Their newly purchased home is in a neighborhood where most of the residents are Black; built in 1913, the old wood-frame house has five bedrooms. They have a new member of the family who is a United States citizen, a granddaughter born in the United States. In Guatemala's public hospitals, Claudia's husband tells me, they don't allow fathers in the delivery room; but here in Pennsylvania he was present when his daughter gave birth. "Seeing a child being born is the ultimate," he says. This miracle they all witnessed was only the most spectacular event in the daily blessing of being a family united in a home where there is safety and work.

Claudia's oldest daughter tells me a story about one memory that stands out in her childhood—the day she turned eleven. The family spent the morning and afternoon walking back and forth across Harrisburg, to get their taxes done, and after several hours of trekking back and forth they were too exhausted to celebrate her birthday. She lived many days like that, the family pulling together on errands that took them back and forth across Harrisburg. "Those are good memories," Claudia's daughter tells me. "Those days of walking in the sun, and in the snow. Because we were together."

I LEAVE HARRISBURG AND CONTINUE MY AUTOMOBILE MARCH westward, crossing the picturesque valleys of central Pennsylvania, and then into the plains of Ohio. Each time I cross the United States, I rush home on the return trip to my home in Los Angeles: I want to make it back to my family in time for Christmas, or the Fourth of July. I buy Christmas presents along the way, or fireworks, and T-shirts that carry the names of the places I've visited, in Iowa, Missouri, New Mexico, and Arizona. Finally I enter the smoggy bowl of the Los Angeles metropolis, the place where all my journeys begin.

Each time I return to my hometown, I understand a bit more about the roads that lead to this place, and the many journeys and diasporas that end here. The largest "Latino" city in the United States feels more vulnerable, more fragile somehow; less an imperial city, and more like the encampments of dozens of different tribes. Los Angeles is a place of wounded people. And it always has been, from the days when it first took that name, to its golden age of real estate booms and film studios, and finally to its dystopian present. Latino is one more story of migration and reinvention, in a city and country founded on the idea of migration and reinvention. From inside the cocoon of my car, the concrete lanes of the exhausted freeway system beneath me, I imagine the denizens of this smoggy bowl huddled in their humble abodes; good people, hardworking, at peril from firestorms and heat waves and earthquakes and plagues. Enduring, and seeking love and shelter, in a city divided ever more between rich and poor, in a nation drifting toward civil war.

CONCLUSION:

UTOPIAS

The promise of a queer future keeps the undocumented, queer young people I've met from going crazy. In the face of the intolerance and weirdness within their own families, and their erasure in mainstream gay and lesbian culture, and the cruelty of the immigration laws of their United States homeland, they embrace the totems and icons of free queer culture. In the stories they write for me, the seer and performer Walter Mercado and his gaudy capes make the occasional cameo, along with the singer Chavela Vargas and her chingona anthems. In their writing my students speak in voices that assert their centrality to American life, even though they are living in a world not yet liberated from the emotional straitjacket of repressed, heteronormative thinking: both "the closet" and "the shadows" loom over their lives.

In a Celia Cruz song that has been adopted as a queer anthem, "La vida es un carnaval," she sings to "all those who think life is unequal," and who "think that all this will never change," with the message that we need to live every moment to the fullest. With our joy we create "a carnival of life" and give ourselves the power to face the cruelties of this world. Celia Cruz's status as a queer icon was cemented by her final performance, a glitzy event staged at the iconic "Freedom Tower" in downtown Miami, an old newspaper building where U.S. officials processed the immigration paperwork of the first generation of Cuban exiles in the 1960s. The salsa singer wore sparkling jewelry and a sequined white silk dress, and her nails were painted white. While her raspy contralto voice blared on the speakers next to her, her folded hands clasped a rosary, and the long curls of her blond wig flowed over the top of her coffin. Celia Cruz was dead. But the accounts of her memorial service would later fixate on the irrepressible energy of the thousands of mourners gathered outside, their dancing and their singing, and the occasional shout of "¡Azúcar!" Celia Cruz's catchphrase, the Miami-Cuban writer and critic Kristie Soares would observe later, embodied a personal philosophy centered on "a relentless dedication to sweetening the present moment."

Celia Cruz was born in Cuba, but it was in the United States, in the latter years of her career, that she became beloved to queer people. She wore huge wigs in tangerine, mauve, and cobalt blue, and ruffled dresses of copious, flowing fabric that became ever more outlandish, until she was finally transformed into the epitome of an Afro-Latinx drag aesthetic. She was a Black woman, she sung in Spanish, and she lives on in the free queer spaces of Miami and many other places, in the poses of the drag queens who smash old and rigid and suffocating ideas of gender conformity, and whose performances are a statement that gender itself is a performance. In 2016, thirteen years after Celia Cruz's death, the horrors of homophobic violence unfolded in an

Orlando nightclub where a gunman killed forty-nine people on its "Latin Night," nearly all of them gay and lesbian and trans people of color. LGBTQ people were reminded, again, of their shared vulnerability. "¡Azúcar!" became a way to mourn, a lament and a chant that expressed the continuity and the resilience of queer life in a world of hate and violence.

"Queerness is not yet here. Queerness is an ideality," the late Cuban American thinker José Esteban Muñoz wrote in his book *Cruising Utopia: The Then and There of Queer Futurity.* "Put another way, we are not yet queer. We may never touch queerness, but we can feel it as the warm illumination of a horizon imbued with potentiality . . . The future is queerness's domain. Queerness is a structuring and educated mode of desiring that allows us to see and feel beyond the quagmire of the present. The here and now is a prison house . . . Some will say that all we have are the pleasures of this moment, but we must never settle for that minimal transport; we must dream and enact new and better pleasures, other ways of being in the world, and ultimately new worlds."

TO LIVE IN THE UNITED STATES OF THE FIRST DECADES OF THE twenty-first century is to see everywhere the evidence of the cruel unwinding of the American project, its unsustainability. I think this when I return to Los Angeles and see the tarpaulin and cardboard constructions of the growing caste of untouchables called "the homeless"; or, in a liberal euphemism, "the unhoused." Or when my television and my computer screens receive videos of routine acts of violence by firearm; when schools, outdoor concerts, and houses of worship open and the season of mass killing begins. Or when I hear news of the tens of thousands of United States residents contributing millions to build "the Wall" in Texas and elsewhere; a secure and confident people do not embrace continent-crossing construction projects to stop nonexistent armies of mestizo "invaders."

The world we live in is "not enough." It is not free enough, it is not true enough for queer people, for the undocumented, and for the millions who call themselves Latinx, Latino, Hispanic. All of us, "Black," "white," "Hispanic," "Asian," and "Native American," live in the quagmire and the prison house of a society built on the deceptions and theft of empire and exploitation. We need to see what young, queer eyes see with clarity: the hypocrisy of the order that aims to contain our free and flamboyant souls, and how we can never be our true selves inside that order.

We attempt to create a new, freer country simply by imagining it, and by enacting a performance of it. The history of the people called "Latino" and of all peoples of color is filled with visionaries whose efforts to remake the United States begin with a meeting, a protest, a poem, or a statement of principles mimeographed in purple ink. Sometimes these activists enter the public eye in the costumes and uniforms of a rebel army—in radical drag, if you will. They remain in character as they march and rally, posing with chins jutted forward in defiance, and slogans on their lips. I'm thinking, of course, of the theatricality of the militants of the Black Panther Party, with their berets and leather jackets, and their weaponry and raised fists. The Panthers spawned many imitators, including, in various Latino and Native American communities, the Brown Berets, the Young Lords, and the American Indian Movement. Groups of men and women who strutted down city streets in formation, or took pictures of themselves holding various firearms, and who did crazy things like taking over islands in the Pacific Ocean, or in San Francisco Bay, proclaiming the ground under their feet liberated territory.

The radicals of the sixties and seventies were flawed people. They produced theories and strategies for revolutions that were often ill-conceived, ridiculous, doomed to failure, and just as often deeply compassionate and forward-looking. Many were emotionally troubled, and in all their groups a male-centered and nationalistic thinking reigned. But their most important and enduring legacy was the performance of rebellion itself. Like a Celia Cruz song, or a drag queen's feather boa, the olive-drab fatigues of the radicals and the rhythms and lyricism of their speeches were an assertion of the liberated possibilities of their people. In El Barrio in New York, the Young Lords appointed a "Minister of Defense," staged a "garbage offensive" of trash barricades to demand better city services, and occupied a church building, demanding food for a hungry community. "When laws do not serve the people and just help the rich get richer, then we must fight to change those laws, not in the courts which they control, but on the streets which we control." The radicals spoke of "struggle" and "colonialism," and their pointed, impassioned arguments and their revolutionary playacting gave their audiences a sense of power and presence. This rush, this injection of adrenaline to a long-suffering community, was a far greater threat to the established order than any weapons they carried or street battles they fought. For every actual rifle they possessed, the Black, and Latino, and Native American radicals of the last century drew pictures and made posters of thousands more. That is why the government and the police forces of the day surveilled them and infiltrated their ranks and tried to crush them, in the same way police with raised batons raided gay clubs and gathering spaces in a bid to destroy even the very idea of gay freedom.

TODAY, MANY OF US CREATE OUR OWN, PERSONAL UTOPIAS with an intimate performance of power and freedom staged for a small audience: the people we love. A young mother goes to work, and she raises her children with a sense of themselves and of their family and neighbors as hardworking, honorable souls. The food she serves her children and the stories she tells them about their past connect them to a history of migration, empire, and resistance. Eventually those children grow up to dance, gather, and march. They seek new ways to transmit the idea of their personal dignity and collective power, to communicate their desires and their aesthetic to their circle of friends, and then to a larger community of viewers, an audience of strangers who tune into their self-produced pronouncements of Latinx, Indigenous, and mestizo joy, pride, and unpredictability.

One morning during the COVID-19 pandemic and its quarantines, my wife shares an Instagram video with me: it shows a Latino teenager dancing on the pitched roof of a home in Inglewood, California. It's the night of the Fourth of July, and as he dances, the sky around him fills with the starbursts of light and fire from the illegal fireworks the locals set off in the Latino and African American neighborhoods around him. The image is one of urban majesty and improvised freedom, and in the text that accompanies his post, the dancer says he is reclaiming the Fourth of July in the name of the survivors of the genocides and displacements that created the United States of America. With each spin and with his raised arms, he declares his ownership of the city and country in which he lives.

Four months later, as the pandemic lingers on, a man from Idaho Falls posts a video on TikTok. In an interview afterward, the creator of this work of art will say he first used the social media platform at the encouragement of his daughter. He lives in a trailer without running water in Idaho Falls, across the street from his brother's house; at one point in his life he'd been homeless, living in a tent on a dirt road along the Snake River. When his car breaks down on the way to his job at a potato warehouse, he takes the longboard he has on his front seat and decides to ride it the rest of the way. On one level, this is a humiliating moment of "precarity," as a social scientist might say, a reminder of so many things that have gone wrong in his life. But he turns on his cell phone camera, and in the video that results, Nathan Apodaca transforms his precarity into something else. Stevie Nicks of Fleetwood Mac sings, and he lip-syncs to her voice. The effect is like that of drag—a juxtaposition of masculinity and femininity. He's the tough-looking dark-skinned guy next door, a "gang member" in the eyes of ignorant strangers. And yet here he is, baring his feminine soul. Underneath the twelve-o'clock shadow on his shaved head you can see the feather tattooed on his skull, which he wears in honor of his Native American mother, a member of the Northern Arapaho tribe. His father is Mexican, and later he will tell an interviewer "I'm Native-Mexican."

The daily performance of mestizo freedom is a central element of United States life—despite the relative absence of that performance in film and television. Mestizo, brown, and Latinx people are reshaping the look, feel, and mood of the country, one video, one front yard, and one street corner at a time. You can see this most obviously in the "rascuache" aesthetic in so many United States cities; the made-up, improvised decorations to be found on homes, automobiles, and businesses. Bright colors, front-yard art made from found objects, Virgins of Guadalupe that light up like Las Vegas signage. The aesthetic of "rasquachismo" is often as garish and loud as drag. As the artist Amalia Mesa-Bains has put it: "In rasquachismo, the irreverent and spontaneous are employed to make the most from the least." You can also see Latinx freedom and assertiveness in the steady stream of self-produced images of personal and family success: a college graduate in her cap and gown, for instance, standing at the edge of an orange grove next to her farmworker parents, dressed in flannel and denim, carrying the bags they use to harvest fruit.

The undocumented undergraduates I've met have told me, more than once, "We are winning the culture war." By this they mean that we are creating in United States culture an image of an American nation with Latinx people in it. They hope that long before they've been granted permanent legal residency and citizenship by Congress, they will have normalized and "legalized" themselves in the eyes of their neighbors.

THE IDEA OF OUR FREEDOM AND POWER MAKES IT POSSIBLE to live and to struggle in a world that devalues us. But how far can the idea and the performance of liberation take us? Can the spectacle of our dancing and our raised fists and our garish homes carry us to a promised land?

In the days when thousands of people were protesting

the public choking torture and murder of George Floyd, there was a fleeting sense that a new world was being born. But as the street uprisings waned, the slogans and symbols of the Black Lives Matter movement were appropriated by corporate America. Professional sports leagues and retailers displayed BLM banners, and the chief executive of the nation's largest bank, JPMorgan Chase, reenacted an iconic ritual of the BLM movement when he joined his staff in "taking a knee" against racism. In the pages of *The New York Times* and other organs of the liberal news media, readers and viewers were treated to one story after another about institutional racism, as a white-centric industry turned its focus to the officially sanctioned barbarity and the everyday humiliations to which Black people are subject. A wry colleague in an American newspaper once told me that "news is what happens where editors live." And sure enough coverage in the *Times* eventually settled into a niche that reflected racial injustices closer to the everyday concerns of the American upper-middle class: stories about the prejudice and the lack of opportunity afforded to assorted professionals, including Asian classical musicians and African American fitness instructors.

In the wake of the George Floyd spring, thinking about racism in journalism and social media became a series of performances of rage and self-reproach. Writers of color and other professionals raised their fists and bared their figurative teeth and excoriated white-dominated institutions for their failure to "see" them; and those institutions bowed their heads and promised "change." These performances betrayed a naivete about racism: they were grounded in a belief that mere attitudes are the problem, and that a country whose institutions have been molded to serve a system of wealth production can somehow be transformed into an egalitarian, race-blind meritocracy. All the while, the basic economic and social structure of the United States remained unchanged and unthreatened. Housing prices continued to soar, the transfer of wealth to an ever-smaller elite was not reversed, the middle class kept shrinking, and Black, Latino, and white poverty did not disappear. And the border fences remained standing and the agents there remained vigilant against immigrant children and their parents.

Race is built into the way our society manages inequality and exploitation. Even if we could swipe the last racist thought from the psyche of every citizen of the United States of America, the need to justify the divisions between rich and poor, between privileged and excluded, would produce new ideas of race and new racisms. This is the essence of United States history, its undying constant. One can imagine a future in which a "multiracial" and "culturally diverse" elite of "white," "Asian," "Black," and "Latinx" cognoscenti enjoys all the pampered comfort of American life, while a mass of impoverished people formerly known as "white" and "people of color" are regrouped into a new "race" of inherently inferior beings with immutable qualities. The process of racializing new groups of poor people is already beginning with the caste of Americans called "the Homeless." Their hygienic practices are questioned, suspicion is raised about their places of origin, their daily habits. As this caste grows, the impatience of the elites with their existence will lead them to be further racialized. A hardened prejudice will form, and more people will see a link between the social standing of the Homeless and the bronzed and wizened skin of their sunburnt arms and faces. Race thinkers will put a pseudoscientific imprint on what many Americans think already: that the Homeless share a biological bent to laziness, alcoholism, and other addictions. And the Homeless themselves will come to embrace the new racial and ethnic identity that has been foisted upon them; already, many call themselves "Travelers," and revel in their status as outsiders, and turn it into a rallying cry. In our lifetimes, the story of "Latino" has been a kind of raciogenesis. New processes of raciogenesis and ethnogenesis await us, the creation of new categories as exotic and ridiculous as the tribes and peoples in a science-fiction epic.

WE CAN'T LIBERATE OUR MIGRANT SOULS BY GOOD FEELINGS alone. Or by Instagram, TikTok, or Snapchat. Or with an op-ed in *The New York Times*. Nor should we aspire to just "fit in," and become cogs in the machinery of profit. We can't simply request "our seat at the table." If we do so we can achieve many personal liberations, while allowing the systems of inequality to reproduce themselves. We must do what we must to survive, to nourish our humanity and raise our families, while also dedicating our energy and our intellects to creating new ways of being in the world.

Race is a story. As I have written here, and as many others have said before, it is a lie at the service of dispossession, inequality, and exploitation. Race is a fairy tale created from the imagination of slave owners and slave traders, and by the leaders of armies bent on conquest and genocide. That story helped build great systems of production that have functioned for centuries, extracting riches from human labor. To each of us, as individuals, the idea that we might one day destroy this matrix of power and profit might seem like pure utopian dreaming. After all, the empire possesses the power of the law and the mass media and the bureaucracies of education and social welfare; it holds many of us in prisons built of concrete, and others in the prisons of poverty and addiction. But we can begin to create a new world with our imaginations. With preposterous visions of unattainable utopias. With ideas and arguments that are as radical, flamboyant, and over-the-top as a drag queen's solo or a Black Panther manifesto, but that spur us to an impassioned, constant, and unyielding effort.

Modern racism feeds off self-interest and individualism. Prejudice is an argument that explains why some live in comfort and others do not. Mass consumerism is an empty, soulless utopia of more, more, and more, of everything— supplied by a global stream of sacrifice and sweat. But a life centered on consumption for its own sake is unrewarding and unviable. Both in a purely mathematical sense, and in the ecological sense, the planet and our brown, laboring bodies cannot sustain the way of life that racism has helped bring into being. Collectively, as a species, we are destroying ourselves with fleets of bloated sport utility vehicles, and with plaster palaces that fill the plains and hillsides of many continents with thirsty lawns and coal-fed power grids. Our grand, utopian visions need to be grounded in a critique of this world. In the disciplined, precise study of the history that brought it into being, and of the contradictions of the present. From this understanding, new movements and new stories will be born. Tales and theories to bring down an empire, setting in motion a true-life epic of human resistance and liberation.

WHEN SOMEONE SEEKS TO QUESTION THEIR GENDER, THEY might stand before a closet filled with clothes, or in a thrift store or a department store. They have come to realize that gender is a performance. We are taught as children to put on this shirt, that dress, this lipstick, those boots, and in so doing we define ourselves as male, female, or something else. But we can choose to change our wardrobe, try on something different, something unexpected. Race is a performance, too. It's a set of clothes thrust upon us, or that we don proudly, a costume pulled off the great thrift-store rack called United States history. But many of us still believe that race is supposed to describe the essence of us, an indelible truth. We can't change our race. So we struggle when the clothes of a racial and ethnic identity don't quite fit us. We decide that just one of these costumes—Black, Jewish, white, Mexican, Asian—cannot possibly capture who we are. We introduce ourselves to strangers with a string of terms, place-names, influences. Our identities are too complicated to fit in one word. Like the university colleague who tells me she is "Cuban and Canadian Irish, from Vancouver." Or like the artist-activist who is introduced before a talk as having an identity rooted in the experience of "being Afro-Peruvian, of being from a family of immigrants, and of being raised in Fruitvale, Oakland," where she was subject to "systemic inequities as a result of being situated in a food desert and in between two major highways."

In the urban districts south of downtown Los Angeles, where African American and Latino people lived side-by-side at the cusp of the twentieth and twenty-first centuries, there are many residents for whom race and ethnic labels are a source of anxiety. In his photo essay on the Blaxicans of Los Angeles, Walter Thompson-Hernández enters into the intimate spaces of young adults with Black and Latino parents. Thompson-Hernández is himself the product of such a transracial union. As a writer for the *Los Angeles Times* put it in a story about him, growing up Blaxican he "navigated Los Angeles with a fragmented lens" and "he had trouble finding a community that represented his whole self." There's a touch of sadness in that description, but there is much more than sadness in Thompson-Hernández's portraits of his fellow Blaxicans. He captures each of them standing somewhere in the greater South Los Angeles landscape, holding old family photographs of their parents. These fading color images are often wedding pictures, and they transport us back into a time when "mixed marriages" were taboo. Thompson-Hernández's subjects hold these old photos in the palms of their hands, and we see the melding of the features of the young bride and groom in the chestnut and mocha faces of their sons and daughters, who look into the camera with varied expressions of pride, hurt, acceptance, and wisdom. Thompson-Hernández's subjects look like survivors of an especially long trek through a race wilderness; after much suffering and contemplation, they have arrived at a destination called "multiracial," and they have found peace there.

We live in a country where "multiracial" people feel they must explain themselves and their place in the race schemes of this country. But really, no explanation is necessary. The United States is a "mulatto" country, and a "mestizo" country, and to be Blaxican is to live the very common and ordinary mixing of distinct "peoples" thrown together by migration and inequality. Blaxican is a way of saying: "We've lived something here together, in this ghetto, in the barrio. And here we became a people." Today, across the United States, we need ideas of identity and struggle that begin with our shared experiences in the places where immigrants and "people of color" and the "unhoused" and "working people" and the hungry and the striving of all "races" meet and mix and form communities together.

In one of Thompson-Hernández's photographs I see a dapper African American man holding his Mexican bride in a 1970s wedding, and I think: I want a theory of social revolution that begins in this kind of intimate space. I want us to create a common language of social change from the stories of our love affairs and our neighborhood encounters. I believe this language is being born, today, in the words we scribble into our journals when we long for connectedness and meaning. In the stories we tell each other about our journeys. In this book, I began with the image of a fair-skinned Guatemalan woman holding her mestizo baby, and I have attempted to build an understanding of the world from the complexity and the beauty of that moment. I am a son of many mixings, from a land of cross-ethnic encounters called "Guatemala," and I am a member of an ethnic group whose newest name, "Latinx," is a synonym for mixed. I want a strategy of change that begins with the idea that community is born from our shared and intersecting experiences of empire and displacement. I want a wardrobe of revolution, costumes of rebellion, sewn from the cloth of the labor we perform each day, side by side. Lifting, scrubbing, folding, writing, counting, teaching, preaching, mothering, hammering, sweeping, cooking.

IN THE MIDDLE SUBURBS OF GREATER LOS ANGELES THERE IS A middle-earth of stucco, weeds, hurricane fences, and concrete. Here, I visit a community that lies on the banks of the cement Rio Hondo River, not far from the site of an old farm camp where Japanese and Mexican laborers lived and struggled side by side, and down the street from the garment factory where seventy-two Thai immigrants were enslaved to work on sewing machines. I find an apartment building there, and when I enter one of the units it resembles very much the apartments I grew up in, many decades ago, in another corner of this metropolis. So much so that I am briefly transported into my seven-year-old eyes, my grade-school longings and anxieties. I have come to interview someone, and when I enter her apartment I find the living room is a space of small rectangularity, with windows facing an asphalt driveway and an asphalt parking area. Once inside I see the sun shining through the bars over the windows, creating parallelograms of shadows on the wall and on the couch. I am greeted there by a woman in her early twenties with wide and intelligent eyes, which are often trained on her two young children.

I'll call her Itzcali, which is a Nahuatl name meaning "house of beauty." She came to the United States when she was eleven with her mother, and in Los Angeles she learned to hide her past from the people she met, with a cover story that explained her Mexicanness: I was born here, in the United States, and then we went back to live in Mexico for a while. Her mother became a street vendor, selling tamales, sandwiches, and champurrado, a drink made of atol de elote and chocolate. She lived among the laboring people of central Los Angeles. Caste status hovered over her growing up, as it does for so many Latino people, documented and undocumented. Would she be condemned to a life among the unseen, the unimportant, the uncelebrated? She was a brown girl being raised by a single mom, and when she was thirteen a cousin told her, "You're never going to graduate high school"; after she got pregnant at age sixteen, several of her relatives embraced that prophecy too. "I knew I was a disappointment to them." The young man who fathered her child could feel the same chains of caste falling upon him, even though he was a U.S. citizen. And that perhaps explains why he told her: *You have to have an abortion. If you don't, I'm going to take our kid from you, and call ICE and have you deported.* (Unfortunately, this is not the first time I've heard of a man using the immigration authorities as a cudgel, and I would guess that every year, across the United States, thousands of boyfriends, husbands, and assorted other cretins make these threats to undocumented women.)

But Itzcali had her baby. She took extra jobs to make ends meet, and even managed to graduate from high school, "with my class," she tells me. But she had still reached a dead end. Or rather, she could see herself becoming trapped by the daily scramble to provide for her daughter and herself. She took a job street vending with her aunt, and she saw herself aging into this work, into the desperate physicality of long days under the sun, hauling the pots filled with her tamales, and the boxes filled with sandwiches from one corner to the next, always with a wary eye for police officers. She moved in with the father of her daughter, and because she was undocumented, she found herself dependent on him in ways that other women would not be. Her paycheck at her new job went to him, because she had to use his Social Security number, and he wouldn't let her drive their car because she couldn't get a license. But then the Obama administration created DACA, and this proved to be her own Emancipation Proclamation.

Armed with a Social Security number for the first time, Itzcali left the father of her daughter and struck out on her own. When I meet her, she's working seven days a week as a food server in an assisted-living facility and as a call-center operator; but she is free. She tells me she is taking classes at a community college, one or two courses at a time, for several years now, making slow but steady progress toward a degree. "From the time I was a little kid, I wanted to be a writer," she says. Her daydream is to write novels about troubled teens like the troubled teen she once was. She found a good man, and married him, and now she reads poetry and a Neruda collection is the newest book on her shelf. Itzcali says she returns home from her classes some nights and opens a book, and her daughter, who is now seven, knows that her mother is studying, and the girl tries to stay quiet during that hour, or two. When Itzcali tells me this I remember being seven years old and listening to my father tell me about his night-school classes, and then leafing through his textbooks, in a small, shoebox apartment that was much like this one. Or maybe exactly like this one.

IN MY MEMORY, AND IN THE PRESENT, I SEE AN ASPHALT "YARD" outside a window, and I hear neighbors' voices, and the carbon of a nearby thoroughfare is a taste in the air. I've been transported into a loop of history, inside a scene I lived a half century ago. Seeing my mother with her legs folded up on a couch like the one in Itzcali's living room, watching my father enter the room with books written by a Nobel laureate. I am in the time loop created by the perseverance of a people today called "Latino," tomorrow called something else. I am inside the cube of an apartment that pulsates with the everyday routines that have allowed generations to survive the hardships of empire and displacement. Cook, study, work, rest. I see family pictures on the wall; a child's bedroom is down the hallway. Before me there is a coffee table and a couch, books on the shelf, and the afternoon sun is making parallelograms on the wall. I have lived this moment before, and I am living it again, and I think of the girl who will take the memory of this room, and of her Latina mother, into a future as yet unwritten.

ACKNOWLEDGMENTS

This book was written thanks to a fellowship from the Radcliffe Institute at Harvard University. While at Harvard, I was assisted by two brilliant undergraduates, Tania Domínguez-Rangel and Jesús Estrada-Martínez.

I owe an enormous debt of gratitude to my longtime partner, Virginia Espino; she directed me to many of the books whose ideas form the spine of the argument of this book, including the work of Nell Irvin Painter, Mae Ngai, Kelly Lytle Hernández, Natalia Molina, and Cheryl I. Harris. Kit Rachlis at the now-defunct *California Sunday Magazine* helped send me on the trip to Guatemala described in this book; and Rachel Poser, then at *Harper's Magazine*, published the story of my journey across the United States. Before that, Dorothy Wickenden and David Remnick at *The New Yorker* published my "Personal History" on living in East Hollywood alongside a white supremacist and a civil rights activist. Many of the ideas in this book were first worked out while writing op-eds for *The New York Times*; thank you, Sewell Chan, for inviting me to write there. Yxta Maya Murray read a first draft of my completed manuscript and gave me some wonderful words of support. Alex Espinoza and Marissa K. López helped get me started on this project when it was the mere germ of an idea. Over the decades I've worked as a journalist, thousands of people have shared stories with me and invited me into their homes; without their trust and generosity, this work would not exist. And finally, I owe a big abrazo to my colleagues and to the students at the University of California, Irvine, for teaching me so much about the Latino present, and for giving me a vision of our Latinx future.

A NOTE ABOUT THE AUTHOR

Héctor Tobar is a Pulitzer Prize–winning journalist and a novelist. He is the author of the critically acclaimed *New York Times* bestseller *Deep Down Dark*, as well as *The Last Great Road Bum*, *The Barbarian Nurseries*, *Translation Nation*, and *The Tattooed Soldier*. Tobar has been a contributing writer for the *New York Times* opinion section and is a professor at the University of California, Irvine. He has written for *The New Yorker*, the *Los Angeles Times*, and other publications. His short fiction has appeared in *The Best American Short Stories*, *Los Angeles Noir*, *Zyzzyva*, and *Slate*. The son of Guatemalan immigrants, Tobar is a native of Los Angeles, where he lives with his family.